Interpreting the Eclipses

Also by Robert Carl Jansky

Astrology, Nutrition and Health
Astrology and the Feminist Movement
Horoscopes — Here and Now
Horoscopes — Musicians and Composers
How to Use the Cell Salts
Interpreting the Aspects
Modern Medical Astrology
Planetary Patterns
Selected Topics in Astrology
Synastry

Also Published by Astro Computing Services

The American Atlas
The American Book of Tables
The American Ephemeris 1901 to 1930
The American Ephemeris 1931 to 1980 and Book of Tables
The American Ephemeris 1931 to 1940
The American Ephemeris 1941 to 1950
The American Ephemeris 1951 to 1960
The American Ephemeris 1961 to 1970
The American Ephemeris 1971 to 1980
The American Ephemeris 1981 to 1990
Basic Astrology: A Guide for Teachers and Students
Basic Astrology: A Workbook for Students

INTERPRETING THE
ECLIPSES

ROBERT CARL JANSKY

ASTRO COMPUTING SERVICES

International Standard Book Number 0-917086-08-2.

Produced by Josh Brackett & Friends.

Printed by Delta Lithograph Company.

Published by Astro Computing Services, P.O. Box 16297, San Diego, California 92116.

Distributed by Para Research, Inc., Whistlestop Mall, Rockport, Massachusetts 01966.

Manufactured in the United States of America.

First Printing, May, 1979.

Few astrologers of today take the trouble to study the major cycles through means of which the ancient biblical prophets were able to foresee the workings of destiny—that man could stay if he would, but seldom does. It is certain that a study of the eclipse cycles, and the application of modern adaptations to the study of the various cycles that were successfully used by the early astrologer-astronomers, will be productive of gratifying results.

—Nicholas Devore in *The Encyclopedia of Astrology*

Contents

Contents

1 ● Cycles within Cycles

We all know people who are skeptical about astrology. "Why," they ask, "do you waste your time studying that superstitious nonsense?" On one quarter we have scientists who tell us that astrology has no scientific basis in fact. From another quarter we hear the religionists who insist that astrology is a tool of Satan and that we are engaged in the devil's work. Much of the general public conceives of astrology as little more than fortune-telling.

Yet at the same time interest in astrology in the United States has never been higher than today. Recent polls indicate that better than sixty percent of those who buy and read a daily newspaper read the astrology column. The polls estimate that better than eighty percent of the adult U.S. population at the very least know their Sun signs. And, somewhere near ten to fifteen percent of the population have taken the time to have their natal horoscopes cast. The astrology industry which includes all money spent by the U.S. population on things astrological, is now well on the way to becoming a $2-billion-a-year industry. This in turn generates approximately $500 million a year in tax revenue at the federal and state level, and it has caused a lot of business people to realize that "thar's gold in them thar heavens!"

This increased interest in astrology has given, I'm sure, many people something to believe in. Scientific technology has not produced the utopia that many people looked forward to; in fact, in many cases it has generated more problems than it has solved. For many others, a kind of blind religious faith with Earth life serving as a kind of kindergarten training for the hereafter is also unsatisfactory. All of us, in one way or another, are looking for a deeper meaning to life, the answer to those great philosophical questions: Why am I here? Where did I come from? Where am I going? We want to believe that all is not chaos and chance in the universe, that there really is some kind of master plan that is being worked out and an order to all things. In the study of astrology it is possible to perceive such order and to predict with great certainty the movement of the heavenly bodies. It is a case of cycles within cycles and fields within fields. When it comes to the study of eclipses this perfect and very predictable order becomes quickly apparent to us today as it was also very apparent to the astrologers of old who indeed, as Devore points out, were able to foresee the workings of destiny through the various cycles in the universe.

The overwhelming majority of persons who express an interest in astrology, for whatever reason, do so on the basis of a different kind of faith. That is, they believe that astrology works even though they can give no rational explanation of why it works. Therefore, astrology is very vulnerable to rational attacks by scientists, such as in the recent articles in *The Humanist*. However, those who attack astrology are just as vulnerable for the most part, be they scientist or religionist, because they have not taken the time to investigate astrology to a point where they have a basic understanding of astrological principles.

The arguments pro and con astrology are *both* as yet irrational because neither side has been able to show in scientific terms that astrology does or does not work. We are only in the very early stages of doing the required scientific studies to prove or disprove astrology. We thus can only theorize. The problem is that astrology's proponents have not been doing enough theorizing lately and many astrologers cannot even remember the last time they actually looked into the night sky to at least remind themselves that there exists a relationship between astrology and what they can actually see!

In this book I am going to do a lot of this kind of theorizing. I do not claim to have any final answers. However, each of us using his own senses can judge to his own satisfaction whether there is a relationship between the planetary cycles and positions and what is happening on a daily basis in our own lives. Therein lies the real proof, I think, at least for the time being.

I am not, however, willing to put this problem down at this point, because I believe that one can construct a very rational theory for why astrology might very well work, and a lot of the evidence is right under the noses of the scientists . For the remainder of this chapter I am going to lay out these facts in an order that makes sense to me and I hope to you. And I am going to do so in simple layman's terms so that we all may understand these ideas a little better.

The Magnet

The magnet and the phenomenon of magnetism were discovered over two thousand years ago, probably by the ancient Greeks. The Greeks found a naturally occurring mineral of natural iron oxide (which we call "magnetite") that when allowed to rotate freely, aligned itself from north to south and also strangely attracted other bits of iron to it. Later, the Portuguese navigators (and probably navigators before them) adapted this mineral and iron itself into the compass for determining directions on both land and water. Just exactly how magnetism works, what it really is, has never been fully explained even by the scientists of today. The fact is, magnetism exists; it works, and it has been put to all kinds of practical uses. Just like astrology?!

Magnetic energy is just one form of a vast spectrum of energy which we call electromagnetic energy. Other forms of electromagnetic energy include infra-red, ultra-violet, x-rays, light rays, radio waves and so on. The ability of these rays to penetrate matter varies with the wave length of the energy. We know, for example, that x-rays have great penetrating power and go right through our bodies, whereas light rays do not. Radio waves and magnetic energy also have great penetrating power, for our radios and TV sets operate inside of our homes. We live constantly in a vast sea of electromagnetic energy every minute of our lives, the constitution of which varies from place to place. And the constitution of this electromagnetic environment directly affects us in many ways. Infra-red rays, for example, cause sunburn. You can't get sunburned in your home; you have to place yourself in an environment where there is a concentration of infra-red radiation to tan your skin, i.e., in the bright sun outside of your house. You can't read where there is no light present.

Where does all of this electromagnetic energy originate? Much of it is of course produced by the Sun, but not all of it. Some originates within the earth itself, like atomic energy from uranium and plutonium, and the Earth's natural magnetic field. A substantial proportion also originates from within our own galaxy of stars, the Milky Way, which scientists tell us has its center at approximately 27° of Sagittarius. This energy is loosely referred to as either "galactic" or "cosmic" energy.

The composition of this field changes from moment to moment due to the movement of all of the planetary and cosmic bodies in our universe. John H. Nelson has shown that the angular relationships of the various planets, one to another, change the radio transmission properties of Earth's ionosphere ("Cosmic Patterns: Their Influence on Man and His Communication"). In the 1950's, Giorgio Piccardi in Florence, Italy, demonstrated that when the Sun is at about 90° from the galactic center of 27° Sagittarius (during its passage through either Virgo or Pisces) the surface tension of water is measurably reduced and its wetting power thus increased. We've also observed that sunspots radically alter the character of the Earth's ionosphere and magnetic field in measurable ways and affect radio transmission. And in the 1930's Takata in Japan demonstrated that the state of the Earth's electromagnetic field also influences the properties of the only substance capable of life, of which we are all composed, protein.

If the weather can influence our personality and behavior, as we've all observed that it does, it is no strain at all on the credulity and logic to understand that a cause and effect relationship exists between the status of our galaxy and solar system and our human behavior. Or, if not a direct cause and effect relationship, at least a correspondence exists between what goes on out in space and what is happening down here on the surface of the Earth.

Whereas many of the changes in the electromagnetic field about the Earth are rather subtle from minute to minute, to have the major source of electromagnetic energy to the Earth suddenly blocked off, either partially or completely, for a short time is anything but subtle. It is drastic indeed, and for the ancients who did not understand what was happening it was traumatic and awe-inspiring. With today's advanced technology we are able to measure some rather vast changes in the character of the Earth's electromagnetic field during this blocking off of the Sun during an eclipse.

It thus does not strain logic too much to at least hypothesize that this drastic alteration in the Earth's field affects, in some subtle way, the workings of the mind and in its intricacy leaves some briefly residual effect upon its operation and functioning.

The Generator

Physicists have demonstrated that whenever an electric current (which is also electromagnetic energy) flows through an electrically conductive material like an electric wire, it sets up a circular magnetic field about the conductor at right angles to the flow of current. Conversely, if one moves a conductive substance through a magnetic field, cutting through lines of magnetic force, one sets up a flow of current through the conductor. It is this latter principle upon which we generate all of the electric current used in our homes and factories. Water, or some other form of power, is applied to rotate a conductor in a magnetic field. This is elementary high school physics today, and it can easily be demonstrated.

The human nervous system consists of nerve fibers connecting various parts of the body together to make it function properly as a whole. These nerve fibers are conductors of tiny electric currents which transmit messages to and from the brain. These currents can be measured using an electroencephalograph and other devices. The lie detector is another instrument for measuring the electrical nature of the surface of the skin.

If current flows through the nerve fibers, then a magnetic field is set up around the body, and it may well be that auras do exist and can be seen by persons having unusually acute visual perception for this type of eletromagnetic radiation.

If eclipses, for example, have such a drastic effect upon the Earth's magnetic field, is it illogical to at least suppose that they affect the body's magnetic field proportionally? And, if all of the more subtle changes in the Earth's electromagnetic field from moment to moment affect our weather and radio transmissions, is it illogical to suppose that such changes affect the character and operational status of our bodies as well? Why do critics of astrology find it so difficult to put all of these facts together and draw their own conclusions!

But, let's get back to the generator. If the nervous system conducts electricity, then every time we move we are cutting lines of magnetic force in the Earth's field and thus we all become generators every time we move. To move is to generate an electrical force over our nervous system. Thus, we are energized not only by the food we eat but by our movements within Earth's magnetic field as well. The character of this energy we generate must be influenced by the character of the magnetic field through which we are moving.

We also know scientifically that the strength and concentration of magnetic lines of force varies from place to place over the surface of the Earth. Thus, the geographic location in which the body cuts through Earth's magnetic lines of force influences body response and energization. Thus, it is not unreasonable to suppose that place of birth and present geographical location could influence behavior patterns, which is what astrology has been trying to tell the world for centuries.

Galvanic Skin Response

An instrument called a galvanometer is used by scientists to measure very weak and subtle electrical currents. When connected to the surface of the skin it shows the electrical nature of the surface of the skin. The lie-detector works on this principle. It measures "galvanic skin response."

Recent medical experiments have shown that the electrical nature of the environment in a hospital room influences the rate of recovery from illness or surgery. A positively charged environment on the skin's surface tends to promote the healing process; a negatively charged environment impedes it.

Elementary physics tells us that we can rub electrons off the surface of certain substances, and when we do we give this surface a positive electric charge. Electrons carry a negative electrical charge and thus tend to be attracted to positively charged electrical surfaces, especially when the air is moist. That is static electricity. When we walk across a rug, for example, we rub electrons off the surface of the body, giving the body a positive electrical charge. In the dry winter environment of the average home the body retains this positive charge until we touch something that has more electrons on its surface than our body. When we touch the object we get a shock as electrons move from the surface of the object to the surface of our skin.

Why does a good hot shower and/or a good massage feel so good and tend to perk up our spirits? Because, in both cases, we are rubbing electrons off the surface of the skin, which makes us feel better. This improved sense of well-being remains until the electron balance has been restored to the skin as the skin picks up electrons from the atmosphere around it. If we eliminate or reduce the available electrons in the environment surrounding the body, as is done in hospital rooms, this sense of well-being is prolonged. It may well turn out that, with all of the interest in pyramidology today, pyramids in some way shunt off electrons and either preserve or create a positive charge on the skin's surface.

The fact remains, however, that a positive electrical charge on the skin's surface improves our feelings at that moment. And it is also a fact that during an eclipse the Earth's atmosphere becomes more highly charged with electrons, creating a negatively-charged environment, which may well account for why eclipses have in the past been given such a negative interpretation.

In summary, it is a demonstrated fact that the electrical nature of the surface of the skin affects our immediate outlook on life, our feelings and our emotions. A rainy day keeps the environment highly conductive and minimizes the possibilities of a positive charge on the skin's surface; a warm, sunny day preserves it.

Fields within Fields

Our solar system is merely one of millions of systems that comprise our Milky Way galaxy. Our galaxy is shaped like the wheel of a wagon with our own solar system located somewhere within the rim of this wheel. It is constantly engulfed by the flow of the cosmic energy streaming out from the center of this galaxy, over and around the Sun and planets of our system. It creates a galactic cosmic field of a certain nature which varies only very subtly.

Our Sun sets up its own electromagnetic field which extends out over our entire solar system. The cosmic field and the Sun's field interact with each other to create varying conditions from moment to moment as they move in space in relationship to one another.

The planetary and asteroid bodies, as they move about the Sun, influence the basic nature of the Sun's field and change its character, since they too are magnetic like the Earth. They absorb and reflect certain forms of electromagnetic energy and thus provide their own characteristic influence based upon their nature and composition.

We know that the Moon, which is so close to the Earth, also influences the character of Earth's environment, as for example its influence on the tides of the ocean.

We also know that the Earth itself influences its electrical environment as it too influences which electromagnetic forces will be absorbed or reflected by its environment.

No two human bodies are exactly alike. Each human body differs somewhat as the result of its basic hereditary makeup and composition. There is a subtle difference in its protein composition. Each human body can recognize its own protein and protein that is foreign to it. This happens through the body's immune system, which preserves it from the attack of bacteria, viruses and other protein foreign to the body's basic nature.

Cycles within cycles, fields within fields, each influencing the nature of the other: the Sun contained within the galactic system; the planets contained within the solar system; the Moon contained within the planetary system; the Earth contained with the Moon's system; the Earth's magnetic field influenced by the greater systems; our own magnetic field influenced by the Earth's magnetic field; our heredity influencing the magnetic field we produce.

Summary

Knowing all of these basic scientific facts, I cannot understand why any competent scientist can continue to insist that the positions of the heavenly bodies have no influence upon human behavior! However, I can understand that there might be a lot of problems in agreeing upon just how the relative positions of these heavenly bodies, one to another, actually influence behavior. The queston is not so much one of *if* but a question of *how*. The remainder of this booĸ is devoted to the study of *how* eclipses influence human behavior, based upon my own personal observations.

2   ●   What is an Eclipse?

At some time in his life, almost everyone has seen an eclipse. If it was a lunar eclipse that you saw, you saw it during the night-time. If it was a solar eclipse you saw it during the daytime, when the Sun was above the horizon. So, we all recognize that there are basically two kinds of eclipses: eclipses of the Moon and eclipses of the Sun.

During a solar eclipse, either a portion or the complete disk of the Sun (as viewed from the Earth) is temporarily blotted out. It is as if some dark body were passing across the face of the Sun and temporarily blocking out the flow of the Sun's energy to the Earth. This "dark body" is the Earth's satellite, the Moon. Where the face of the Sun is blocked off totally, we call this a total eclipse of the Sun. Where only a portion of the Sun's disk is blocked, we call this a partial eclipse of the Sun.

As astrological students we know from our basic studies

that when two heavenly bodies appear to occupy the same place in space they are said to be conjunct to each other. Thus, a solar eclipse can only occur when the Sun and the Moon are conjunct in space, at a particular degree of some sign of the zodiac. We commonly refer to a conjunction of the Sun and Moon in space as a new Moon. Thus, a solar eclipse can only occur at the new Moon. However, there is at least one new Moon every calendar month, and we know that there is not an eclipse each month (usually there occur only two solar eclipses each calendar year); so something else must be involved here making the solar eclipse a rather special kind of new Moon when it occurs.

During a lunar eclipse, either a portion or the complete disk of the Moon is temporarily blotted out. Again, it appears as if some dark body in space were moving between the Moon and Earth to blot out the Moon's light. Here again too, the Moon's light may be blotted out completely or only partially, so we have the phenomena of either a partial eclipse or total eclipse of the Moon.

Unlike the Sun, the Moon does not generate radiant energy of its own. What we see on Earth as the Moon is really light bouncing off the Moon's surface, reflected toward Earth, that originates from the Sun. At those special times when the Sun, the Earth and the Moon are aligned in space in a straight line with the Earth in the middle, the Sun's light traveling toward the Moon's surface is blocked off. The black circle that appears to be traveling over the surface of the Moon is really the Earth's shadow being cast upon the Moon.

During this special alignment the Sun and Moon appear to be directly opposite in space to each other, in the same degree but in opposite signs of the zodiac as seen from the Earth. Thus, a lunar eclipse can only occur when the Sun and Moon are in opposition to each other. We commonly refer to such an opposition as the full Moon, which we know from our calendar normally occurs at least once each calendar month. But we also know that there is not a lunar eclipse each month, so a lunar eclipse must be a special case of a full Moon with some other factor operating as well to cause the eclipse.

If we turn to an authoritative reference book that lists the dates for solar and lunar eclipses we quickly discover several very interesting facts. We are able to predict the dates on which eclipses will occur many years in advance, so we must therefore conclude that eclipses occur in some predictable and cyclic way. In fact, we not only can predict the date of occurrence but also the exact time and the exact zodiac location, by sign and degree, where they will occur.

The next thing that we discover is that eclipses seem to occur about every 169½ days for solar eclipses, or about six lunar months apart. Furthermore, we discover that solar and lunar eclipses seem to occur in pairs, with the lunar eclipse occurring either fourteen days before or fourteen days after the solar eclipse. We also note that there are occasional solar eclipses that occur without any accompanying lunar eclipse, but the converse is not true. There can never be a lunar eclipse without an accompanying solar eclipse.

Now let's investigate and discover what those special factors are that separate the solar eclipse from all of the other new Moons.

Declination and Latitude

The equator is an imaginary line drawn around the center of the Earth. All points on the equator are equidistant from the true poles of the Earth upon which the Earth appears to be rotating. If we just extend this equatorial circle out from the Earth and project it upon the sphere of the heavens, we refer to it as the *celestial equator*. There is another circle that we can draw in the heavens about the Earth: the path over which the Sun appears to travel during its yearly revolution of the Earth. The Romans called this path the *via solis*; in modern-day terms, we call this path the *ecliptic*.

The celestial equator and the ecliptic do not coincide but instead are tilted at an angle of 23°27' to one another. These circles do touch at two points: 0° Aries, the first day of spring,

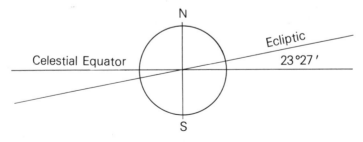

Figure 1

and 0° Libra, the first day of fall, both dates being the time that the Sun is on the celestial equator.

When we normally speak of the position of the planets, Sun or Moon in astrology, we are concerned with where in the circular orbit of the particular body it is located at a given time. We are not concerned with whether the planet is above or below the celestial equator, merely where it is located in its orbit. We describe its position in terms of degrees and minutes of a particular sign; e.g., 5° Cancer 31′, and speak of this position as the body's *longitude.*

None of the planets follows a path in space that coincides with the celestial equator; thus, all have orbits that are inclined to the celestial equator by some angle. During half of their orbital period they are above and during the other half they are below the celestial equator.

Thus not only can we describe a celestial body by its longitude (sign position), but we can also describe its position in distance above or below the celestial equator in degrees and minutes north or south of the equator. This position is called the body's *declination.* The body's declination on any given day can be determined from the ephemeris by looking at the declination table. The closer to Earth a body is, the faster its declination changes, with the declination for the Moon changing very rapidly and the declination for Pluto changing very slowly.

If, instead of using the celestial equator as our measuring point for this "up and down" motion of the bodies, we use instead the ecliptic, then instead of a declination measurement we get the planet's *celestial latitude.* Latitude is expressed in terms of minutes and degrees north or south of the ecliptic, and can usually also be found for any given date in most ephemerides.

Astrologers do not make much use of latitude positions of the planets; however, they do use declination measurements in several important instances. Declinations are important when we are concerned with the aspect called the *parallel.* The parallel aspect occurs when two planets are within 1° of the same degree of declination.

The parallel aspect is also most important in the consideration of eclipses. For an eclipse to occur, the Sun and Moon must be not only conjunct or opposed to each other but also at the same time parallel to one another. This is what makes the eclipse a special type of new or full Moon, for this parallel does not always occur when the Sun and Moon are conjunct or opposed to one another.

The Moon's Nodes

There is still another condition that must be met in order to have an eclipse. In simple terms, not only must the Sun and Moon be conjunct or opposed and in parallel aspect, but both bodies must be conjunct one (solar) or both (lunar) of the Moon's nodes.

Most ephemerides give the mean position of the Moon's north node on a daily basis with the Moon's south node assumed to be at the same number of minutes and degrees but in the opposite sign.

The north and south node for any planet or the Moon are the two points in space where the orbit of the planet or Moon intersects the orbit of the Sun (the ecliptic). For the Moon, this point moves about 0°3′ backwards through the zodiac per day. For a node to make one complete revolution of the zodiac it takes approximately 6585.36 days or a little over 18 years. For the rest of the planets, their nodal position moves ever so slightly on a yearly basis. Surprisingly, perhaps, this information was known quite accurately by the ancients. We will discuss this information more fully later when we come to the section on the Saros cycles, but for now let us be content with knowing just this much information.

The Eclipse Limits

Rarely do the positions of the Sun, Moon, and north or south node of the Moon *exactly* coincide in space during an eclipse. They come close to each other, but they are usually not exact. Thus we must ask the natural question, how close is close? Obviously there must be some limit beyond which an eclipse cannot occur. These limits are as follows.

Total Solar Eclipse For a total solar eclipse to occur, the Sun and Moon may not deviate more than 9°55′ from the Moon's nodal point. It must occur if they are within this orb. It can, but does not always occur, when the orb is between 9° 55′ and 11°15′.

Solar Eclipse Limits A solar eclipse can occur when the orb from the Moon's node is ±18°31′ or less. It must occur if the orb is ±15°21′ or less. If the orb is 9°55′ or less the eclipse will be total. Between 9°55′ and 11°15′ it can be either partial or total. From 11°15′ to 18°31′ it must be a partial eclipse.

Total Lunar Eclipse   When it comes to a lunar eclipse, the orbs are somewhat smaller. For a total lunar eclipse to occur the Sun and Moon must be 3°45′ from the Moon's nodal point or closer. A total eclipse must occur if they are within this orb. It can but does not always occur when the orb extends to ±6°0′.

Lunar Eclipse Limits   A lunar eclipse can occur when the orb from the Moon's node is less than 12°15′. It will occur if the orb is less than 9°30′. From 12°15′ to 6°0′ it will be a partial eclipse. Below ±3°45′ it must be total. Between 3°45′ and 6°0′ it can either be partial or total.

Occultations

As it is possible to have an eclipse involving the Sun and Moon—the two luminaries—it is possible to have an alignment in which either the Sun or Moon interposes itself directly between the Earth and one or more planets. Such an occurrence is usually referred to by astronomers as an *occultation* rather than an eclipse, a term they tend to reserve for the Sun-Moon-Earth combination.

Just how important, if at all, such occultations are has been a subject of considerable controversy among astrologers for a considerable period of time. One of the leading proponents for their importance in delineation has been Charles Jayne. Other astrologers question the importance of occultations in delineation. In this book, I do not propose to settle this controversy. To date my own observations do not provide me with any noticeable effect in my own life or in the lives of my clients from occultations. This is not to say that Jayne is incorrect; rather, the effects of occultations, if any, tend to be quite subtle at best, rarely having any correspondence to important events in the life of those whom I have closely observed.

This question, however, opens up a broader question in astrology which I cannot bypass here. It is rarely spoken of in the current literature of astrology, and yet it goes right to the very heart of matters astrological. We might call this controversy the *ray theory* versus the *perturbation theory*.

Max Heindel was one of the leading proponents of the ray theory in the early nineteen hundreds. Under this theory it is held that it is the actual electromagnetic rays from each of the planets, proceeding from that planet to our immediate body, that affect our total physical, mental and spiritual makeup and behavior. All of those astrological textbooks that refer to the "rays" of each planet as they affect us tend to conform to this theory. It strains my credulity to believe that these people are correct, but I am certainly willing to keep an open mind on the topic.

Under the perturbation theory, rays have nothing at all to do with behavior of individuals. Rather, it is the way in which the movement of the planets about the Sun disturb, or "perturb", according to the physical nature of the perturbing body, the combination of the Sun's and the galactic electromagnetic field. It is like throwing a pebble upon the smooth surface of a lake, and as Pascal says: "The entire ocean is affected by a pebble." The pebble perturbs the water, sends out a ripple effect, and in turn affects everything on and within the water. The effect may be obvious and massive if the pebble strikes an amoeba or other one-celled animal, or it may be very subtle, causing a slight shift of sand particles on the shore of the lake. However, massive or extrmely subtle, the effect is there and can be observed by anyone clever enough to observe it.

Under the ray theory, obviously, the occultation of a planet should have a quite marked effect upon everything that momentarily loses contact with its rays. Under the perturbation theory, we might still expect to see some subtle effect from this momentary cutoff, but certainly not a momentuous change in the life of individuals who experience it.

Perhaps an occultation does in some way alter, temporarily, the vast electromagnetic field in which we live. But, if it does, the effect would seem to be much more subtle than the massive change caused by the Sun-Moon eclipse whose temporary effect is certainly much more observable.

I leave it to you to observe the effects, if any, upon your own life of occultations of the various planets. From this point on, we shall be dealing only with that special kind of occultation which we call the eclipse and with effects that can be observed by anyone with the will and curiosity kind of occultation which we call the eclipse and with effects that can be observed by anyone with the will and curiosity to observe them.

Summary

In this chapter we have tried to collect all of the obvious and observable effects of eclipses. No complex scientific theories here—just facts that either we ourselves can observe or that we can easily obtain from standard scientific references.

We know basically what an eclipse consists of when viewed in astrological terms.

A Solar Eclipse
►is a conjunction of the Sun and Moon
►can only occur at the time of the new Moon
►can only occur when the Sun and Moon are parallel in declination as well as conjunct
►can only occur when the Sun and Moon are conjunct one of the Moon's nodes, within quite rigidly established limits of orb.
►has effects upon the Earth's electromagnetic field that can be scientifically measured
►occurs in cycles and can be accurately predicted
►can be either partial or total.

A Lunar Eclipse
►is an opposition of the Sun and Moon
►can only occur at the time of the full Moon
►can only occur when the Sun and Moon are contraparallel in declination as well as opposed; i.e., one in north and the other in south declination
►can only occur when the Sun and Moon are conjunct the Moon's nodes within rigidly established limits of orb
►has effects upon the Earth's electromagnetic field that can be measured scientifically
►occurs in cycles and can be accurately predicted
►can be either partial or total
►can only occur approximately fourteen days before or fourteen days after a solar eclipse.

There is still a lot more to learn regarding the nature of eclipses. In the following chapters, we will add to our basic knowledge of eclipses by personal observation and by closely studying a table of data relating to Twentieth Century eclipses.

3 ● More on Eclipses

To understand the phenomenon of the eclipse as it relates to astrological delineation, we must first achieve the understanding that the astronomer of today and the astrologer-priests of ancient times had achieved of eclipses.

One of the first concepts that must be understood is the relative sizes of the Sun, Earth and Moon. The Sun's diameter is about 866,400 miles. The Earth's diameter is given as 7,926 miles, while the Moon's diameter is 2,160 miles. If you think of the Moon's diameter as one unit, then the Earth's diameter is equal to 3.67 and the Sun's diameter 401.11. That is to say, the Sun's diameter is about 401 times longer than the diameter of the Moon.

Because the Sun is so large, when the Earth passes between the Sun and Moon it is not difficult to see that the Earth does not cast a very large shadow area. When the situation is reversed, with the Moon passing between Earth and Sun, the

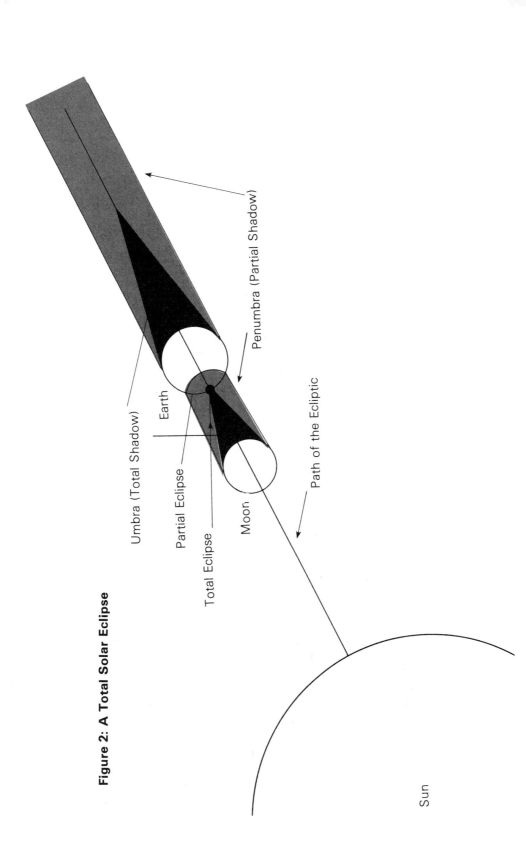

Figure 2: A Total Solar Eclipse

Penumbra (Partial Shadow)

Path of the Ecliptic

Umbra (Total Shadow)

Earth

Partial Eclipse

Total Eclipse

Moon

Sun

Moon being even smaller than the Earth, the shadow cast by the Moon is even smaller than that cast by the Earth.

In a three-body situation such as this, we obtain two kinds of shadows. There is a small area of complete shadow or darkness, which physicists call the *umbra*. Then there is also a much larger area of partial shadow, which physicists call the *penumbra*.

Solar Eclipses

In figure 2, note that the umbra is conical in shape and comes to a focus or point. Whenever there is a total solar eclipse, the Moon's umbra (area of complete blackness) covers a small area on the surface of the Earth. The maximum possible diameter of this area is 167 miles. Usually it is considerably less. It is at maximum diameter if at the time of the total solar eclipse the Moon is at perigee (as close to the Earth as it can get). The Moon's umbra travels along the surface of the Earth at a speed of 1,060 to 5,000 miles per hour, which is why scientists who study eclipse phenomena often track the umbra from a jet plane.

Scientists have measured the length of the Moon's umbra and have found it to be 232,000 miles. The distance from the Earth to the Moon varies as the Moon's orbit is not circular but eliptical. At its closest point to the Earth (perigee) the Moon's distance is 222,000 miles. At its maximum distance from the Earth (apogee) it is 258,000 miles.

This raises an interesting question. What happens when an eclipse occurs while the Moon is at apogee? Because the length of the Moon's umbra is only 232,000 miles and the distance from Earth to the Moon at apogee is 258,000 miles, the Moon's umbra does not strike the surface of the Earth at all. It will be about 26,000 miles out in space above the Earth's surface. In this case the Earth passes only through the Moon's penumbra whose diameter is about equal to the diameter of the Moon.

In this special situation, you can see the totality of the eclipse if you are directly beneath the Moon's umbral point in space. From this vantage point the Moon's surface is not large enough to blot out the entire disk of the Sun. The Sun appears as a bright ring around the black disk. This special case is-called an *annular* eclipse. The picture on the cover of this book is of an annular eclipse.

During the period of totality darkness falls and the electrical character of the Earth's near cosmic field is drastically altered. Birds fly about excitedly, night creatures come out of their dens, predators howl, roosters crow, diurnal animals go to sleep and flowers close their blossoms. In the later chapters of this book we will concern ourselves with what the eclipse appears to do to us as humans, since it affects our biomagnetic fields too.

During a total or annular solar eclipse the eclipse will appear to be total only as long as the observer is within or directly beneath the Moon's umbra. If the observer is within the Moon's penumbra the eclipse will appear to be only partial. If the observer is outside of the penumbra he will not see the eclipse at all, although the temporary alterations in the Earth's magnetic field will in some way affect or influence every living being on the Earth. By contrast, everyone on the night side of the Earth will be able to see a total lunar eclipse provided the Moon is above the horizon at the time.

A solar eclipse begins as the Moon begins to move across the face of the Sun, always from west to east. It was at this precise moment that the ancient astrologer-priests drew their horoscopes and made their forecasts. Finally, as totality is reached temporarily, the stars and planets appear in the heavens. Totality may last for as long as 7.5 minutes, but 4 to 5 minutes is about average. As totality passes, the Moon's shadow cone continues to move east until it finally disappears.

Both modern and ancient mundane astrologers believe that the area of the Earth's surface that lies in the path of the Moon's umbra is where the eclipse will be most strongly felt. Ancient history is filled with stories of how eclipses ended battles and wars and how they were supposed to signify the birth of a king or other person of great importance.

Accurate records of eclipses have been kept since ancient times. The Austrian astronomer Theodor Oppolzer (1841-1886) compiled a catalog of approximately 8,000 solar eclipses and 5,000 lunar eclipses dating back to 1207 BC with the umbral tracks that they produced on the Earth's surface. He was able to predict the exact time for each eclipse within 2 seconds and its umbral pathway within less than a quarter of a mile. Today, the United States Naval Observatory in Washington, DC provides us with this data.

Below is a list of particularly long-duration total solar eclipses that will occur in the remainder of the Twentieth Century. The solar eclipse of June 8, 1937 at 18° Gemini was 7 minutes 13 seconds long, the longest in 1,200 years. The shortest eclipse of the Twentieth Century was on July 20, 1963, lasting only 65 seconds.

Date	Duration	Geographical Location of Umbra
26 February 1979	3 min	From Washington, across the northern U.S. to Greenland
16 February 1980	4 min	From Central Africa to India
11 June 1983	5 min	From the Indian Ocean, across Indonesia and into the Coral Sea
11 July 1991	6 min	From the Marshall Islands, across central Mexico and down into Brazil
3 December 1994	4 min	From East Indies, across Australia, to Argentina
26 February 1998	4 min	From Central Pacific, across Venezuela and out into the Atlantic Ocean

Lunar Eclipses

When we begin to try to understand lunar eclipses we find ourselves dealing with quite a different set of phenomena. In the first place, a lunar eclipse is of much longer duration generally than a solar eclipse and can last as long as two hours. This is because the Earth's shadow cone is about 5,700 miles wide and the Moon's average speed is about 2,000 miles per hour.

With the average length of the Earth's umbral shadow in space approximately 857,000 miles, and the Moon's greatest distance from Earth only about 258,000 miles, there is no possibility of an "annular lunar eclipse." It is either total or it is partial; there is no other possibility. There is however, another phenomenon that is often overlooked in the eclipse tables, what astronomers call an *appulse*. When the orb between the Moon and its node exceeds 12°15' no eclipse can occur; however, it is still possible for the Moon to pass through the Earth's penumbra. This will not produce an eclipse, but it will produce a distinct darkening of the Moon's surface. During the appulse the body of the Moon receives the light of the Sun from only one side of the Earth. The appulse does make a drastic change in the appearance of the Moon.

During its exposure to the Sun, the temperature of the surface of the Moon gets well above the boiling point of water (212 °F). On its dark side the temperature quickly drops to about -225 °F. Since the Moon has no atmosphere to help it retain heat this temperature change occurs very rapidly, at the rate of about 100° per hour. It rises with even greater speed once the sunlight returns. The Moon absorbs about 93% of the Sun's energy it receives and reflects only about 7% (its "albedo"). Nevertheless, the darkening of the Moon's surface during an appulse can be seen, and this phenomenon still embodies both the gravitational effect of the parallel aspect and the interference with the Moon's radiation that we get during a lunar eclipse. In its quantitative effect, I would rate the appulse at about the same level as a partial lunar eclipse. In doing very accurate research work on lunar eclipses, the dates for appulses must also be considered.

In some years, like 1969 and 1980, there are no lunar eclipses at all. This is, of course, not the case with solar eclipses where there must be at least two each year.

Unlike the solar eclipse, the direction of the lunar eclipse formation is from east to west, and as pointed out earlier in a total eclipse it proceeds much more slowly toward totality, and the period of totality lasts much longer.

A curious fact about the Moon is that, despite its albedo (low reflectance), from its sunlit side it reflects infra-red light that is several times more intense than the rays it reflects in the visible light range. During a lunar eclipse the reflection of infra-red radiation ceases completely. One can only hypothesize about what the eclipse does to the Moon's reflectance of other cosmic waves in the electromagnetic spectrum such as x-rays and radio waves.

Are lunar eclipses as important as solar eclipses in horoscopic delineation? One is tempted at first to say no, because the effects of a lunar eclipse on the flora and fauna of the Earth are not so obvious. However, the Moon is our nearest neighbor in space, and we certainly know that the Moon plays a vital role in horoscopic delineation as a kind of interpreter, timer and lens of external cosmic phenomena. It vitally affects our weather, so why should a lunar eclipse be of any lesser importance when it comes to interpreting eclipse phenomena? I think that the major difference in delineating solar and lunar eclipse phenomena astrologically is that the effect of the solar eclipse is much more overt and obvious. The effect of the lunar eclipse, when it accompanies the solar eclipse, is far more covert and subtle. The lunar eclipse works much more at the subconscious level.

It has been shown that at the time of the full Moon, and especially during a lunar eclipse, the surface tension of all fluids is increased (the molecular cohesive forces at the surface of any fluid). Because our bodies consist largely of water, this increase in molecular tension is bound to produce a biochemical effect upon our bodies. Furthermore, our bodies tend to take on and hold larger quantities of water during the full Moon phase each month. The skull, being the only area of the body that cannot readily expand with increased fluid pressure, therefore exerts greater pressure upon the brain cells which ultimately affect our behavior patterns. This increased fluid pressure in the body also explains why there is greater potential of hemorrhage following surgery at the time of the full Moon. For those interested especially in this phenomena, I have included an extensive medical bibliography at the end of this book.

Yes, lunar eclipses certainly are important. They must be considered in any responsible delineation of eclipse effects. In general terms, we are going to discover that it is the position of the lunar eclipse in the horoscope that subtly and subconsciously influences the more overt expression given to the position of the solar eclipse. However, before we go on to the delineation of the eclipses, there is one more piece of scientific information that we cannot overlook, which I will discuss in the next chapter.

4 ● The Saros Cycles

Reliable records of eclipses have been kept since about 747 BC, the beginning of the reign of Nabonassar. In the British Museum are to be found a number of these ancient records. One is carved on a large stone taken from Nineveh which lists the lineage of kings and eclipses that occured during their reigns. Based upon these early records, those who followed were able to perceive the cyclic nature of eclipses. A vastly important discovery was made by the Chaldeans: *Saros cycles*. The word Saros simply means "repetition" in the language of the ancient Babylonians. With the discovery of these cycles it became possible to predict eclipses accurately years, even centuries, in advance.

This discovery made it possible for Cidenas in 383 BC to accurately measure the synodic month as being 29.5 days and the tropical year as being 365.25 days. He also found that an eclipse returns to its same place in the heavens after every 223 lunations. Thus he determined the length of a Saros cycle to be 6,585⅓ days, or 18 years, 9-11 days (depending upon the number of leap years in the interval). There is some evidence that the Chaldeans knew of this Saros interval even earlier in the Sixth Century BC.

Even earlier than Cidenas, the Greek astrologer Meton had noticed another less precise cycle, later referred to as the Metonic cycle. Meton noticed that in intervals of 19 years from the precise date in each year there would occur another eclipse in approximately the same degree of the zodiac. He discovered this in 432 BC in Athens. The problem was that Meton's cycles were not precise enough, since approximately 23 per cent of all eclipses have no Metonic return.

Thus, it was early observed that eclipses come in predictable cycles. A complete series of Saros cycles consists of seventy or seventy-one solar eclipses and lasts for a period of about 1,260 years with a period of 6,585⅓ days between two successive eclipses in the same series.

The seventy to seventy-one cycles in the Saros series follow a very predictable pattern. The first eclipse in the series commences as a tiny solar eclipse at either the north or south pole. It is always partial. Subsequent solar eclipses occur farther from this pole as the series progresses. Toward the middle of the series the eclipses commence becoming total as their route over the Earth's surface takes them farther from the pole where they started and closer to the equatorial latitudes. Later after a series of annular and total solar eclipses, the eclipses begin to get progressively more partial again, the last in the series occurring at the opposite pole from which it started.

Because of the one-third day in the 6,585⅓-day timing of each eclipse return in the Saros series, each successive eclipse appears 120° farther west than its predecessor, as the Earth has turned one third of a revolution from the last eclipse location. After each three eclipses the position returns to the original longitude again but at a latitude either farther south or north, depending upon at which pole the series started.

This predictable movement is shown in figure 3. Note that the interval between succeeding eclipses in the series is about 18 years and a few days, that each eclipse occurs about 120° west of the preceeding eclipse, and that with each eclipse the succeeding member in the series is at a lower latitude.

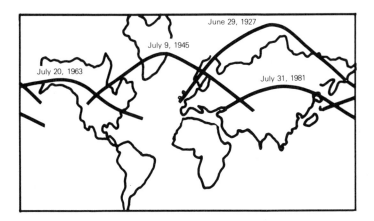

Figure 3

Astronomers have identified thirty-eight Saros series of solar eclipses and thirty-eight Saros series of lunar eclipses, all of which are presently in various stages of commencement or completion. I will shortly identify these for you.

The lunar eclipses also occur 6,585⅓ days apart, with either forty-eight or forty-nine lunar eclipses occurring over a period of 865 years. Actually the lunar eclipse series is longer; about the same length as the solar series. The difference between the 865 years (lunar) and 1,260 years (solar) is that each lunar series actually begins with about eleven appulses (see Chapter 3) or penumbral lunar eclipses preceeding the first partial lunar eclipse in each series. You will recall that in an appulse the Moon passes only through the Earth's penumbra so that there is no shadow on the Moon's surface; only a visible darkening.

Interpreting Saros Cycles

You may well ask the question at this point, Why have I gone into the Saros cycles in such detail? The information is nice to know and certainly valuable to astronomers, but why is it important to the astrologer? There is a very important reason for understanding the Saros series. *The ancient astrologer-priests used these cycles in their predictions.* To understand the importance of the Saros series in their historical perspective, we must return to the time of Ptolemy.

In evolving his system of predictive astrology, Ptolemy had several goals: first to identify geographically which cities and kingdoms would be affected by a solar eclipse, second to predict the time of occurrence of the eclipse, and third to establish the period of time the eclipse effect would last. This was a mundane-oriented, rather than a person-oriented, astrology.

As to the geographical location and effect of the solar eclipse, Ptolemy was less interested in the path that the Moon's umbra would follow across the surface of the Earth than in the sign location in which the eclipse occurred and its relationship of the ascendant, midheaven, Sun and Moon in the horoscope of the city or kingdom. Ptolemy correctly reasoned that an eclipse might well affect in some way all locations on the Earth's globe.

As to the duration of effect, Ptolemy incorrectly (I believe) reasoned that the duration of effect of a solar eclipse lasted as many years as the eclipse lasted in hours, and for the lunar eclipse as many months as the eclipse lasted in hours.

Once this had been determined, Ptolemy next turned his attention not only to the sign location of the eclipse but also to which star or planet in the heavens the eclipse occurred closest to, and he gave this body rulership over the eclipse. He also concerned himself with the stars or planets that were on the eastern and western horizons at the time of totality. Using the symbolic rulership of these bodies he then proceeded to determine what classes or kinds of things were most likely to be influenced by the eclipse. He also took the time of year of occurrence into consideration. For example, an eclipse close to the Spring Equinox was said to affect the germination of seed and bud development, or an eclipse close to the Autumn Equinox, the yield of the harvest and the flocks.

Ptolemy had the benefit of the writings of Hipparchus, who preceded him by about two centuries, and the benefit also of historical records of previous eclipses from the Babylonians, Chaldeans and Egyptians. Thus he knew of the Saros and Metonic cycles and was able to make one of the important discoveries of this earlier period regarding the Saros cycles.

This rule of interpretation was that *each succeeding eclipse in a particular Saros series took on the nature of the sign in which the first eclipse in the series occurred*. For example, if the first eclipse in the newly formed series occurred in Aries, then every eclipse that followed in the series was Arian in nature with all that the symbolism of Aries implied. Thus you can see why the various Saros series were considered so important: because it was important to determine the exact sign location of the first eclipse in the series.

In the Appendix to this book I have included a table of all of the eclipses that will occur during this century, along with the Saros series in which each occurs. Certain of these series, for example series 2, are unusual. Since 1928 and continuing through the year 2000, every time there is a series 2 solar eclipse a second solar eclipse occurs 28 days later. This is why there can be as many as five solar eclipses in one year.

The Saros series do not occur one after the other. That is, as one series is drawing to a close the next series has already started to form. Take, for example, the 1928 north nodal solar eclipses which occur 28 days apart. On May 19, there is an eclipse at 28° Taurus. This is the last of the total eclipse that will occur in that series which started on June 24, 792 o.s. On June 17 there was another partial solar eclipse at 26° Gemini, one that occurred at the very tip of the north pole, that is the start of a whole new Saros series. As one series is drawing to a close, another new series has already started to form in most cases.

I think you can now see why I have devoted an entire chapter of this book to the Saros cycles and series. My observations indicate that if we are to understand the nature of the eclipses that we are delineating in the horoscope, then we must first know the nature of the Saros series of that eclipse. From the table in the Appendix, you can identify the particular series of any eclipse, and from the following descriptions for each Saros series determine something of the astrological nature of the particular series. In the following we shall be concerned only with the solar eclipses.

Saros Series 1

The North Nodal Series This series commenced on January 4, 1639 at 13° **Capricorn**. Thus all eclipses in this series are of the nature of this sign and degree. The first total eclipse in the series occurred on June 6, 1891 at 16° Gemini, and the total eclipses in this series will continue to occur well into the Twenty-first Century. They will all occur at the

Moon's north node. The next eclipse in this series will occur on July 31, 1981 at 8° Leo. It will be total.

The South Nodal Series This is a separate series in Saros cycle 1 from the above, and all eclipses will occur at the Moon's south node. The series commenced on August 24, 1729, at the **Leo/Virgo cusp**. Until 2126, all solar eclipses in this series will be partial. The next eclipse in this series will occur on January 25, 1982, at 5° Aquarius.

Saros Series 2

The North Nodal Series This series commenced on June 24, 792 o.s. (June 28 n.s.) at **6° Cancer**. The total eclipses in this series started on July 18, 936 o.s. and continued until May 19, 1928. The current series is now ending with a series of final partial eclipses; it will end with the eclipse of August 3, 2024. Meanwhile a new series has commenced with the first partial eclipse of June 17, 1928, at **26° Gemini**. Successive eclipses in this new series occur on June 29, 1946, July 9, 1964, July 20, 1982 and July 31, 2000. For the next hundred years all eclipses in this series will be partial.

The South Nodal Series This series started on April 17, 991 o.s. (April 22 n.s.) at **2° Taurus**. The total eclipse phase commenced on July 12, 1135 and continued on until October 10, 1874. It is now in the final partial phase and will end in the Twenty-first Century, accompanied on each occasion by a total lunar eclipse.

Saros Series 3

The North Nodal Series This series began on October 10, 991 o.s. (October 15 n.s.) at **22° Libra**. The total eclipse phase began on May 14, 1352 o.s. and will end on August 15, 2091. All eclipses in this series are currently total and of long (4 to 5 minute) duration having no accompanying lunar eclipse until 1947.

The South Nodal Series This series commenced on August 13, 1208 o.s. (August 20 n.s.) at **27° Leo**. The total eclipse phase began on March 17, 1569 o.s. (March 27 n.s.) and continues through the Twentieth Century in a series of annular eclipses with accompanying partial lunar eclipses.

Saros Series 4

The North Nodal Series   This series began on May 25, 1389 o.s (June 2 n.s.) at **11° Gemini**. The total eclipse phase began on August 20, 1533 o.s. (August 30 n.s.) and continues into and through the Twentieth Century in a series of eclipses that start out as annular and end as total as the Moon's umbra finally touches down on Earth's surface during totality. After the May 9, 1948 eclipse in this series there is no longer an accompanying lunar eclipse or appulse in this series.

The South Nodal Series   This series started on April 17, 1624 at **27° Aries**. The total eclipse phase commenced on July 3, 1750, and continues well into the Twenty-first Century without an accompanying lunar eclipse after October 7, 1930.

Saros Series 5

The North Nodal Series   This series commenced on October 12, 1516 at **19° Libra**. Throughout the Twentieth Century it continues as a partial eclipse, always accompanied by a total lunar eclipse. It begins its total eclipse phase on May 31, 2003.

The South Nodal Series   This series started on July 14, 1784 at **22° Cancer**. It will begin the total eclipse phase on November 2, 1967 and continue it well through and beyond the Twenty-first Century. Meanwhile, an earlier series in the last partial eclipse phase was ending with its final eclipses on August 31, 1913 and September 12, 1931. Each of the Twentieth Century solar eclipses is accompanied by a total lunar eclipse.

Saros Series 6

The North Nodal Series   This series began on May 15, 850 o.s. (May 19 n.s.) at **28° Taurus**. The total eclipse phase commenced August 20, 1012 and ended with the total solar eclipse of March 18, 1950. From this date on, each of the later partial solar eclipses will be accompanied by total lunar eclipses well into the Twenty-first Century.

The South Nodal Series   This series began on March 6, 1049 o.s. (March 12 n.s.) at **22° Pisces**. The total eclipse phase began on June 12, 1211, and ends with the total eclipse of October 3, 1986. The final partial eclipse phase proceeds on into the Twenty-first Century.

Saros Series 7

The North Nodal Series   This series started on October 3, 1103 o.s. (October 10 n.s.) at **17° Libra**. The total eclipse phase commenced on May 6, 1464 o.s. (May 15 n.s.). All of the Twentieth Century eclipses in this series are annular eclipses and have no accompanying lunar eclipse. Both the north and south nodal eclipses in series 7 are currently of interest to astronomers becuase they are of long (4 to 5 minute) duration.

The South Nodal Series   This series began on June 22, 1248 o.s. (June 29 n.s.) at **7° Cancer**. The total eclipse phase commenced on October 9, 1428 o.s. (October 18 n.s.) and all of the Twentieth Century eclipses in this series are annular with no accompanying lunar eclipse until the September 23, 1987 solar eclipse, which is accompanied by a partial lunar eclipse, beginning a new series of lunar eclipses.

Saros Series 8

The North Nodal Series   This series began on May 17, 1501 o.s. (May 27 n.s.) at **6° Gemini**. The total eclipse phase began on August 11, 1627, and all of the eclipses during the Nineteenth and Twentieth Centuries were total and accompanied by partial lunar eclipses through the solar eclipse of March 7, 1970. Thereafter there is no accompanying lunar eclipse.

The South Nodal Series   This series started on April 1, 1718, at **11° Aries**. The total eclipse phase began on July 7, 1880 with a series of annular eclipses extending through the Twentieth Century, all accompanied by partial lunar eclipses.

Saros Series 9

The North Nodal Series   This series commenced on August 8, 528 o.s. (August 10 n.s.) at **17° Leo**. The total eclipse phase began on April 15, 907 o.s. (April 20 n.s.) and continued through the eclipse of July 12, 1646. This series ended with the partial solar eclipse of January 5, 1935. Meanwhile, a whole new series commenced on August 21, 1664, at **28° Leo**. The total eclipse phase of this new series will begin on April 9, 2043. Thus, all of the eclipses in this series during the Twentieth Century will be partial.

The South Nodal Series This series began June 23, 727 o.s. (June 27 n.s.) at **5° Cancer**. It became total with the eclipse of October 10, 907 o.s. (October 15 n.s.). This phase ended with the eclipse of May 6, 1845. The series ended with the partial eclipse of July 22, 1971. Meanwhile, a whole new series commenced with the partial eclipse of July 19, 1917 at **26° Cancer**, and the total phase will commence with the eclipse of October 3, 2043. All of the Twentieth Century eclipses in this series are accompanied by a total lunar eclipse.

Saros Series 10

The North Nodal Series This series began on April 25, 944 o.s. (April 30 n.s.) at **10° Taurus**. The total eclipse phase commenced on July 10, 1070 o.s. (July 16 n.s.) and it will continue until February 28, 2044. All of the Twentieth Century eclipses in this series are annular with an accompanying total lunar eclipse.

The South Nodal Series This series started with a partial eclipse on March 10, 1179 o.s. (March 17 n.s.) at **26° Pisces**. The total eclipse phase started on June 4, 1329 o.s. (June 12 n.s.) and it will end on August 23, 2044. All of the Twentieth Century eclipses in this series are total and accompanied by a partial lunar eclipse.

Saros Series 11

The North Nodal Series This series started on August 1, 1125 o.s. (August 8 n.s.) at **16° Leo**. The total eclipse phase began on March 27, 1522 o.s. (April 6 n.s.) and will continue throughout the Twentieth Century with a series of annular eclipses and no accompanying lunar eclipses.

The South Nodal Series This series commenced on June 14, 1360 (June 22 n.s.) at the **Gemini/Cancer cusp**. The total eclipse phase began on September 8, 1504 o.s. (September 18 n.s.), and all of the Twentieth Century eclipses in this series will be total with no accompanying lunar eclipse.

Saros Series 12

The North Nodal Series   This series began on May 19, 1613 at **28° Taurus**. The total eclipse phase began on August 4, 1739. All of the Twentieth Century eclipses in this series are annular.

The South Nodal Series   This series began on September 19, 1541 o.s. (September 29 n.s.) at **6° Libra**. The series ended on April 8, 1902. A second series began on February 12, 1812 at **23° Aquarius**, and its total phase began on May 29, 1938. In the Twentieth Century the eclipses in this series after April 8, 1902 were all in the second series.

Saros Series 13

The North Nodal Series   This series began on August 14, 1776, at **21° Leo**. During the Twentieth Century all of the eclipses in this series are partial and accompanied by a total lunar eclipse. The total eclipse phase in this series will commence on February 28, 2101.

The South Nodal Series   This series began on May 24, 803 o.s. (May 28 n.s.) at **6° Gemini**. The total eclipse phase began on August 18, 947 o.s., and ended with the annular eclipse of April 29, 1957. The May 11, 1975 and May 21, 1993 eclipses are partial, and the series will end on July 14, 2083. This series will not repeat itself for many years. All of the Twentieth Century eclipses will be accompanied by a total lunar eclipse.

Saros Series 14

The North Nodal Series   This series started on April 29, 1074 o.s. (May 5 n.s.) at **15° Taurus**, and the total eclipse phase began on July 2, 1182. This phase ended with the total eclipse of October 12, 1939. The eclipses of October 23, 1957, November 3, 1975 and November 13, 1993 are all partial. Commencing with the 1957 eclipse, all accompanying lunar eclipses are total.

The South Nodal Series   This series started on August 29, 984 o.s. (September 3 n.s.) at **10° Virgo**. The total phase began on May 16, 1417 o.s. (May 25 n.s.). During the Nineteenth and Twentieth Centuries all eclipses in this series are annular.

Before the April 19, 1958 eclipse, they had no accompanying lunar eclipse. From 1958 on they are accompanied by partial lunar eclipses. The total phase will end on July 25, 2120.

Saros Series 15

The North Nodal Series This series began on July 13, 1219 o.s. (July 20 n.s.) at **27° Cancer**. The total eclipse phase began on November 30, 1453 o.s. (December 9 n.s.) and continues as total solar eclipses throughout the Twentieth Century, each time without an accompanying lunar eclipse.

The South Nodal Series This series began on June 6, 1472 o.s. (June 15 n.s.) at **24° Gemini**. The total eclipse phase commenced on August 31, 1598 and will continue throughout the Nineteenth and Twentieth Centuries as a series of annular eclipses, each with an accompanying partial lunar eclipse.

Saros Series 16

The North Nodal Series This series began on February 25, 1599 n.s. with a partial eclipse at **6° Pisces**. The total eclipse phase began on June 24, 1797 and continues through the Nineteenth and Twentieth Centuries as a series of total eclipses accompanied by partial lunar eclipses through the total eclipse of September 21, 1941. After this eclipse the total eclipses are unaccompanied by lunar eclipses.

The South Nodal Series This series began on September 21, 1653 n.s. at **28° Virgo**. Throughout the Nineteenth and Twentieth Centuries it continues as a series of partial solar eclipses all of which are accompanied by total lunar eclipses. The total solar eclipse phase will not begin until April 29, 2014.

Saros Series 17

The North Nodal Series This series started on July 1, 680 o.s. (July 4 n.s.) at **12° Cancer**. The total eclipse phase began on October 7, 842 o.s. (October 11 n.s.) with a long series of annular eclipses that ended with the eclipse of May 27, 1816. All of the Twentieth Century eclipses in this series are partial with the series completely ending with the brief partial solar eclipse of August 12, 1942. Meanwhile a second new series commenced on July 28, 1870 at **5° Leo**. The Twentieth Century eclipses in this new beginning series were on August 20, 1906, August 30, 1924, September 10, 1942, and all dates beyond. All of the eclipses in the Nineteenth and Twentieth Centuries (for both the beginning and ending series) were accompanied by a total lunar eclipse.

The South Nodal Series   This series started on May 27, 933 o.s. (June 1 n.s.) at **12° Gemini**. The total eclipse phase began on August 11, 1059 o.s. (August 17 n.s.) and continues through the Nineteenth and Twentieth Centuries as total eclipses, this phase ending with the total eclipse of March 30, 2033. All of the Nineteenth and Twentieth Century total solar eclipses are accompanied by partial lunar eclipses.

Saros Series 18

The North Nodal Series   This series began on February 4, 1060 o.s. (February 10 n.s.) at **21° Aquarius**. The total eclipse phase began on June 13, 1276 o.s. (June 20 n.s.) and has continued through the Nineteenth and Twentieth centuries as a series of annular eclipses. This phase ends with the annular eclipse of August 22, 1979, and the final partial phase commences with the partial solar eclipse of September 1, 1997. Until the annular eclipse of August 11, 1961 each solar eclipse was accompanied by a partial lunar eclipse. However commencing with the 1961 annular eclipse, the next eclipses in this series are accompanied by total lunar eclipses

The South Nodal Series   This series began on August 20, 1096 o.s. (August 26 n.s.) at **3° Virgo**. The total solar eclipse phase began on April 5, 1475 o.s., (April 14, n.s.) and continues through the Nineteenth and Twentieth Centuries as a series of total eclipses, all of which are unaccompanied by any lunar eclipse.

Saros Series 19

The North Nodal Series   This series began on July 5, 1331 o.s. (July n.s.) at **21° Cancer**. The total solar eclipse phase began on October 21, 1511 o.s. (October 31 n.s.). This phase continues through the Nineteenth and Twentieth Centuries as a series of annular eclipses, and after the annular eclipse of June 6, 1872, it is unaccompanied by a lunar eclipse.

The South Nodal Series   This series began many centuries ago (date unfortunately uncertain). Through the Nineteenth Century it proceeded in a series of total eclipses until November 30, 1872, when the total eclipses began to convert over into annular eclipses. All of the Twentieth Century eclipses are annular and unaccompanied by lunar eclipses.

The above descriptions of the various Saros cycles should be used along with the Table of Eclipses for the Twentieth Century in the Appendix in studying the nature of any eclipse that you are delineating.

Both historical and modern observation seems to confirm that the astrological strength of any eclipse depends upon its completeness. An annular eclipse being stronger than a partial eclipse and a total eclipse being stronger than an annular eclipse. This applies to both solar and lunar eclipses.

As pointed out earlier, the zodiacal longitude at which each series began has been said since ancient times to color the effect of all eclipses in the entire series. Whether or not the zodiacal longitude at which the total eclipse phase began has an "overlay" coloration of the series is a subjective judgement which I leave to the individual astrologer doing the delineation. It is my strong impression that such an overlay effect does exist and ought to be considered.

5 ● Delineation

In this chapter I want first to give you an overview of the various factors that enter into the delineation of an eclipse. Now that we have developed an understanding of how the astronomer views an eclipse, we are ready to examine eclipses from an astrological point of view as they might apply in doing a natal delineation or progressed forecast.

House Position

As one begins to delineate the horoscope for the effect of an eclipse, the single most important factor to note is, In which of the twelve houses does the eclipse fall? *It will be in terms of this house that you will feel most personally affected by this eclipse.*

When the eclipse falls on one of the intermediate house cusps, i.e., a house cusp other than one, four, seven or ten, the question is raised, Which house system do you use in delineating the eclipses? I personally prefer the Koch system of houses because it tends to be the most accurate in placing an eclipse in the area of life that comes under the focus of the eclipse.

The keywords to apply to the delineation of an eclipse are *emphasis* and *crisis*. The eclipse tends to emphasize matters in relation to the house which it falls in the horoscope. The eclipse tends to bring matters related to this house to a crisis stage during its period of effect. The word "crisis" is not a malefic word, if you look it up in your dictionary. It simply means that you are required by events in your life to devote more time, attention and energy to some matter(s) than usual. Herein, I believe, you will discover the very essence of the importance of the eclipse in delineation.

If you do not know the time of birth of a particular individual, inquire into what it is that is currently occupying the most time, attention and energy, in his/her life at the moment. Then place this crisis properly by house, and you have a rough indicator of how the chart is arranged by signs on the house cusps. We will discuss this in greater detail later.

When you have an eclipse that is very close to an intermediate house cusp you have a fine opportunity to judge which house system best fits your horoscope. This is done by simply judging what crisis in your life at that time comes closest to the choice of the two houses facing you, and then selecting which of the two houses best fits the situation and finding a house system that places the intermediate cusp properly either before or behind the eclipse position to fit the situation.

In your delineation of the area of crisis or emphasis, be sure to consider some of the more obscure meanings of the house involved. There have been many instances during my astrological practice in which a client could not initially relate to the house emphasized by the eclipse. However, upon more careful questioning, it was easy to establish this link. Let me cite several examples to illustrate this.

One client who had the eclipse emphasis currently in the seventh house reported a very serious crisis with one of her children. It was clear that this was the most important problem in her life at that moment. Children are, of course, a fifth house matter. However, the problem was with her

second-born child which, upon rotating the chart is specifically a seventh house matter.

A second woman with an eclipse emphasis in her fifth house
was severely grieving over the loss of her dog, a French poo-
dle, whom she has raised from a pup. Normally, dogs and pets
are a sixth house matter; however, it later showed that this
woman had no children and treated her dog as she would a
child if she had had one. Pets treated as child-substitutes are
more a fifth than a sixth house matter.

A man with an eighth house eclipse emphasis was involved
in the final stages of a divorce from his wife, normally a
seventh house matter. Upon more careful questioning it was
revealed that the cause of the divorce was his wife's frigidity
and inability to have a satisfactory sexual relationship with
him. The eighth house symbolizes what we expect from our
partner in the sexual relationship.

Another man with a ninth house eclipse emphasis was also
involved in the final stages of a divorce. In this case it turned
out that the cause of the divorce was that his wife was
suspected of having an affair with the man's priest! Clergy are
a ninth house matter.

Conjunct or Opposed Planet

What if the eclipse position is conjunct (or opposed to) the
position of a planet in the natal horoscope? Limiting the
allowable orb in such an instance to $\pm 5°$, the answer is that
usually the crisis or emphasis tends to take on more major proportions; i.e., it becomes a more "major" crisis. A number of
authorities suggest that you look at all major aspects to the
eclipse position. My personal observation is that better than
ninety percent of the individuals for whom you delineate will
only be able to relate to crises represented by conjunctions or
oppositions to this point. After all, eclipses deal exclusively
with conjunctions and oppositions. It is only the most highly
evolved individuals who can relate to squares, inconjuncts,
sextiles and trines to eclipse points.

Saros Series

The basic nature of the Saros series of the eclipse must be considered in making your delineation. That is to say, the sign

location of the first eclipse that occurred in the Saros series. In the aforementioned example of the man with the ninth house eclipse, he was under the influence of the April 29, 1976 annular eclipse at 9° Taurus. This is in Saros series 14 at the south node. This series began at 10° Virgo (see chapter 4). Ten degrees of Virgo fell in his first house, conjunct his ascendant. Those with Virgo rising tend to idolize their partners and find it difficult to see any wrong in them. Apparently all of this man's friends knew what was happening between his wife and the priest before he did. When he finally admitted to himself what was happening and was confronted with the evidence, the divorce became a matter of personal pride with him (a first house matter).

While the divorce was the crisis of the moment for this man, its cause was a ninth house matter, but the underlying cause could easily be related to the nature of the Saros series of the eclipse under the influence of 10° of Virgo, which fell in his first house. The basic nature of the Saros series involved in the eclipse yields added information to the delineation. In this case, making the divorce a matter of personal pride and ego.

Fixed Stars

The basic nature on any fixed stars that are conjunct ($\pm 5°$) the eclipse position should also be considered and the basic nature of that star as to the influence, if any, it might exert over the eclipse. In the above case, the eclipse of April 29, 1976 at 9° Taurus 20 ' was within the orb of conjunction with the fixed star Almach at 13° Taurus 7 '.

Almach, ruled by Venus, is one of the few purely benefic fixed stars, according to De Luce. It is ruled by Venus. The man's wife was an artist, and Venus occupied his seventh house in Pisces. His divorce went very smoothly with no hitches. The almach is a small Arabian animal like a badger, and it was this man himself who unearthed the truth for himself, badger-style, by waiting in hiding to discover the truth.

Rising or Setting Stars

The basic nature of any fixed stars just above the eastern or western horizon should also be considered in interpreting the full meaning of the eclipse. In the case of this man, the fixed star Skat was just above the western horizon in his natal chart in April 1976 at 8° Pisces 32'. Skat was conjunct the planet Venus.

According to Keane, this conjunction with Skat "denotes one who may be defiant and belligerent because of his/her own inherent weaknesses which are realized subconsciously...and hidden from the Self as well as the rest of the world." From all accounts this description would adequately describe the man's wife, which is not at all surprising since the conjunction with Skat is in the man's seventh house.

Rarely have I ever seen this factor considered in any modern delineations of the effect of eclipses. The ancients used it, and I think that in our studies we should at least give it a fair try. In many cases I have studied, it at least gives color and added background detail to the delineation. A list of the longitudinal positions of the major fixed stars is included in the Appendix for your reference.

Planetary Ruler

If a planet other than the Sun or Moon is conjunct (orb ± 5°) the position of the eclipse at its time of occurrence, it is said to be the planetary ruler of that eclipse. Such planetary rulers will also tend to color the delineation you give to the eclipse.

In the example case we have been mentioning, the April 29, 1976 eclipse had such a planetary ruler. It was the planet Jupiter, located at 8° Taurus 20' in a tight 1°10' orb with the eclipse point at 9° Taurus 20'. Jupiter too was located in the man's ninth house. The ninth house, of course, includes many things, including in-laws and long-distance travel as well as the lessons we learn from experience. In this case, perhaps rather suprisingly, the man got great support from his in-laws during the divorce proceedings (because the wife's parents thought the actions of their daughter wrong), and the priest resigned his position in the church and took a long trip overseas where he reportedly visited the Vatican to seek forgiveness for his indiscretions. This man, now sadder but wiser for the experience, has vowed on several occasions that he will not rush into marriage again when he thinks that he's found the ideal wife. And, as pointed out previously, the divorce went very smoothly for him with no hitches, Jupiter being the "greater benefic.'' During the eclipse period, he too took an ocean voyage to Mexico following the granting of the divorce.

As we shall point out in the next chapter in greater detail, ninth house eclipses are frequently involved in the pursuit of freedom from someone or something. Certainly this applies to the case we have been examining. Ninth house eclipses also refer to the knowledge we gain from listening to what others have to say. Perhaps this man would have been better advised to seek out and listen to the knowledge that his friends had discovered before him regarding his wife and pay attention to the knowledge that they could have imparted to him.

I could relate many other cases in which all of the above factors figured prominently in the delineation of the problem. They are all important when you wish to study the particular eclipse effect in greater detail.

Path of Umbra

Mundane astrology teaches us that the nations and peoples living in the geographical regions traversed by the umbra of the solar eclipse are most strongly influenced by that eclipse. It seems logical to me that this is true since the effect of the eclipse ought to be most dramatic for those people and nations in the effect the eclipse produces upon their biomagnetic fields, and thus upon their nervous systems. In a detailed study of eclipse effects upon the psychology of the individual and national entity, the path followed by the umbra of the eclipse certainly must be considered.

Summary

In this chapter I have outlined for you all of the astrological and astronomical factors relating to solar eclipses that I consider to be of greatest importance. These are summarized below. In the following chapters we shall take up some of these individual factors in much greater detail.

In analyzing the eclipse, you should ask yourself the following questions:

►In which house in the horoscope under study does the eclipse fall? What are the keywords for this house polarity?

►Does the eclipse fall in conjunction or opposition to a natal point in this chart (orb ±5°)?

►To what Saros series does the eclipse belong? What is the basic nature of this series as determined by where the first eclipse in this series occurred?

►Does the eclipse fall in conjunction to the position of one of the fixed stars? What is the basic nature, astrologically, of this fixed star and what planet is its ruler? Where does this planet fall in the horoscope?

►At the exact time of this eclipse, were there any fixed stars just above ($\pm 5°$) the eastern or western horizon? What is the basic nature of these fixed stars?

►Does the eclipse have a planetary ruler (does it fall within $\pm 5°$ of some planet's transiting position on the date of the eclipse)?

►Did the umbra of this eclipse pass over the geographical area in which the individual under study either lives or was born?

►Was the eclipse itself partial, annular or total? What is your overall assessment of the strength of this particular eclipse upon the life of this individual?

►For what period of time will this particular eclipse affect the life of the individual?

All of these question are important! You cannot do an in-depth investigation of any eclipse until you have answered all of these questions. In the next chapter we will begin to investigate the first question in more detail.

6 ● The Import/Export Game

No man is an island. The Christian religion stresses our responsibility each one of us for the other. Biologists tell us that man, like so many other species of animal, is a social being and must cooperate one with the other for the survival of the species. Humanistic psychology stresses the incompleteness within ourselves that each of us feels which motivates us to reach out into our surrounding environment for that which we sense will help us to achieve completeness.

Astrology also teaches this principle through the symbolism of Jupiter and Saturn, the Sun and the Moon, principally. Jupiter is the outreach into the external environment to add to ourself what it is that we sense we lack, and this process results in expansion and growth. Saturn represents the price we must pay for this expansion and growth, what we must give in order to get. For that which we attempt to import we must be willing to export something else in return. The symbol for the Sun is a dot within a circle. The dot represents the core of our individuality and the circle the space that we occupy. As we know, some individuals occupy more space than others, so the space within the circle varies from individual to individual. The more we take in or import, the more space we require to hold the imported material. This process is perhaps best illustrated in the process of human development from the fertilized ovum that occupies only a microscopic portion of space to the space occupied by the matured adult.

Psychologically, as we begin to sense a need and desire for greater space, we all ask ourselves:
►Is the particular space worth occupying?
►Is it relatively safe to occupy that space, or will there be opposition from others to occupy the space too?
►Can I safely defend that space, once occupied, from attack?
►To what purpose will I put this space, once I occupy it?

The symbol for the Moon is a crescent. It is this testing process that goes on before the space is actually occupied. The Moon is our scout that precedes the main body. It is also the decision-making process which is highly conditioned by past experiences and events, habit patterns, etc. Thus, in dealing with the delineation of the eclipses, we are concerned with this need to occupy greater space, the reasons for it, and all of the testing that preceeds the actual process of occupation.

We could spend considerable space in this chapter discussing the esoteric meaning of the various planetary symbols, but other authors have already done this very well. I will not attempt to repeat their work. But, just to complete this picture I will again mention briefly the role of Mercury, Venus and Mars in this process. Venus, the pleasure principle, symbolizes the enjoyment of the space that we occupy. It is the injunction to "stop and smell the flowers," to appreciate what we already have, in the struggle to hold and gain more space. Mars is the symbol of the actual struggle to hold what we occupy, to defend our space from attack and to expand it. Mercury, with the crescent Moon above the circle and cross, is our awareness of this human struggle for more space, the pleasure it will give us to occupy more space and all of the planning that must first take place before we (the Moon) sally forth to bargain for, or test the defenses of, the space we intend to occupy.

Just to complete this planetary picture, Uranus would be the voluntary relinquishment of certain space (two crescent Moons pulling inwards upon themselves), one step backwards in order to later take two steps forward. Neptune represents the dream we have for ourselves, the ideal in the achievement of all of the space we could need or want and its ideal usage once occupied and Pluto represents the elimination of all of the junk presently occupying that space that prevents its complete enjoyment and development.

We shall soon discover that when an eclipse transits the natal position of one of these planets, whatever process the planet represents gets accentuated in our life at that time. For example, a solar eclipse conjunct natal Sun greatly accentuates the desire to expand the space currently occupied.

The Import/Export Principle

No nation is complete unto itself, not even the United States, though it is indeed richly endowed in natural resources. America must trade with other nations that occupy space containing resources that the United States lacks.

As the need for trade and exchange is the natural function of nations, it is the natural function of all life. Ideally, such exchange or barter should take place easily, with each party recognizing and supplying the needs of the other, but in practice such is not the case. There are problems. Exchange of natural resources involves risks to both parties in the trade if one party determines that the risk in trading a certain commodity is too high, trade cannot occur. The risk involved is generally assessed in terms of the potential threat to space occupied. For example, the United States will not trade atomic weapons with the Soviet Union, for to do so would provide the Soviet Union with sufficient power to threaten the space occupied by the United States. War results when two nations refuse to barter with each other and one of these nations attempts to take the resource it wants from the other by force; i.e., Mars.

There is another danger in import/export. It is the danger of over-closeness and dependence. The danger is loss of autonomy. No nation and no person wants to openly admit to the world its weaknesses; nevertheless, we all have them, none of us being perfect or complete within ourselves. Any legal contract, be it a national treaty or a marriage, implies the recognition of individual weakness in some regard and an alliance to bolster up this weakness. Something is sacrificed for the potential gain to be realized from the transaction, with both parties hoping that the gain is greater than the loss.

Thus in all barter transactions, there is a balance to be maintained. Both parties to the transaction must be willing to take certain inherent risks for the possibility of gain. Unwillingness to take risks thus prevents expansion into greater space and the threat of loss of space presently occupied.

Complementation

Psychologists use the term "complementation" to describe this import/export principle as it applies to individual human beings. The dictionary defines it as "a process which fills up, completes, or brings something to perfection...the act of completing a set...something added to complete the whole." The idea of complementation is not a difficult concept. In fact, it is made easier to understand if it is viewed as a person importing what he needs from another person or group of persons while exporting what those persons need in return.

Most people consciously or semi-consciously realize the need to carry on this import/export at a very early age. From the moment that the umbilical cord is cut at birth there is at least a primitive realization that now no longer will all of the needs of the individual be automatically met. The baby cries when it is wet, cold or hungry. Later, the growing child learns that to get what it wants it must do something in return. For example, to get an allowance from its parents, the child must perform some chore or conform to some desired behavior pattern.

In this growing process the child also realizes that there are inherent risks in this process, and the game becomes one of, How can I get the greatest return for the least amount of sacrifice?

Eric Berne, in his book *Games People Play* provides us with examples of the many variations that there are in the playing of the import/export game. We might very well retitle his book, "Import/Export Games People Play." The whole field of transactional analysis in psychology is built upon the import/export principle.

The import/export principle is also quite adequately

demonstrated in the symbolism of astrology. Since we are dealing here with the expansion of space occupied, the addition of greater space external to ourselves, the taking of resources from the environment, it should not surprise you to learn that it is from the symbolism of the houses in the horoscope that we can delineate how each of us plays the import/export game on a personal basis.

The Principle of Astrological Polarity

Just as no individual exists as an entity unto himself, no astrological sign, house or planet exists symbolically as an entity unto itself. Each has its antithesis or polar opposite. One cannot, for example, fully understand what black is without some understanding of its opposite, white. The concept of good cannot be fully understood without an equal understanding of its opposite, evil. This is the yin/yang principle.

To be fully understood, astrological symbolism also requires a comprehension of polar opposites. One cannot, for example, fully comprehend the meaning of pleasure (Venus) or appreciate it fully without some understanding of its opposite, pain (Mars). Communication is a two-way street; it requires someone to do the speaking (ninth house) and someone to do the listening (third house). Things that are of positive value (assets) have no value at all unless we are equally able to understand those things that have negative value and are really liabilities to us (the Taurus/Scorpio principle).

All of us have had the experience of being asked, as students of astrology, for example, "I am an Aries. Tell me about myself." And if you have chosen to fall into this trap, as most of us have from one time to another, and rattled off some of the characteristics of the Aries-type individual, you can relate to the response from that individual who replies, "Your description does not fit me at all!" If astrology really has a relationship to the realities of life, then astrology must be able to account for these differences from the symbolic prototypes. Fortunately, when we fully comprehend the astrological law of polarities, astrology does account for these variances. And at the same time it also accounts for free will in any course of action we choose to pursue.

Figure 4: The Aries/Libra Spectrum

Using the diagram above, let us suppose that in your natal chart you have Mars located in Aries. Hereditarily you were born with Mars in the Aries/Libra spectrum (about which you can do nothing). How you choose to use your physical energies (symbolized by Mars), however, is up to you. Let us assume that at an early age you chose point 1. This represents a rather aggresive expression of these energies. However, as you grow older, you discover that to be so aggressive causes you discomfort in your relationships with others, who resent such aggressiveness. Therefore, you adjust to social conditions and choose to be less aggressive, moving to point 2 in the spectrum. Subsequent experience later dictates that point 2 is also uncomfortable because now you find others running roughshod over you. So you again adjust to a more comfortable position, point 3.

Let's take another example, that of a person with Sun in Aries. Let us suppose, as happens with some frequency, that one day you discover a book on astrology and read the delineation for Sun in Aries. You say to yourself, "That's not me at all! I'm not egotistical. I try to be considerate of the feelings of other people. Sure, I like challenges, but when I respond it's always done in the spirit of good fun. I don't necessarily get, nor want, my own way all the time." Should you therefore conclude that astrology is "for the birds?" Let us hope not! However, if astrology is to be of value to you it must be able to account for this anomaly. Fortunately, astrology does provide a very adequate answer to this problem when one understands the law of polarities. However, it requires that we stop thinking of people in terms of signs and start thinking of them as individuals who are free to express their talents, energies and total makeup in the way they choose to do so. That is to say, we must be willing to deal with shades of gray.

Scientists speak of energy (which all of the planets represent) as being either potential or kinetic. Kinetic energy is energy in motion; potential energy is energy at rest or stored. In delineating a chart we must always consider planetary energies as being kinetic. Part of the maturation process of each individual is learning where in this spectrum for each of the planets the energy is best expressed, the point that at a given moment gives us the greatest pleasure and the least pain. Shifts toward one or the other extreme though usually subtle are constantly being made as we adjust to life's changing conditions. Point 3 may have been very comfortable at an earlier age, but perhaps now a point closer to point 1 is more comfortable.

If you begin to view the expression of planetary energies in these terms, the old astrological controversy of determinism versus free will becomes moot. Each of us is born with a certain potential, as shown by the natal chart. Heredity establishes certain limitations for all of us. The man who is five feet six with brown eyes and black hair may wish to be six feet tall with blue eyes and blond hair, but he never will be. If you were born with your Sun in Aries—or more precisely, in the Aries/Libra spectrum—there is nothing you can do about it. What you *can* do, and here is where free will enters in, is to choose where within this broad spectrum you wish to express your individuality and all else that the Sun symbolizes.

Many people and organizations today offer to interpret your natal horoscope by mail without ever meeting with you in person. Under these conditions they cannot possibly determine how, at the moment, you have chosen within the established spectrum to express each planetary energy in your life. The best they can do is to describe the typical individual, if such exists, having the same set of astrological circumstances. Therefore, to get a meaningful interpretation of your natal horoscope an in-person meeting and exchange of information between client and astrologer is a must. Before your astrologer can really be of help to you the astrologer must determine where in the spectrum for each planet you are currently expressing this energy. And perhaps one of the greatest benefits to be derived from an astrological consultation is to discover how to shift your position in each planetary spectrum in order to get yourself in a more comfortable balance with current conditions.

House Polarities

This same basic principle of astrological polarity applies to opposite houses as well as to opposite signs. Each house pair deals with the same specific circumstances of life, but from opposite extremes. And it is through the houses that we see the import/export principle in action in our lives.

Once we have come to the realization that we are not complete in ourselves, that there are things that we have in abundance to give and things that we lack, it becomes necessary to take inventory of ourselves. The question becomes, What do I want, and what am I willing to trade for it? Everything we seek to get from outside of ourselves costs something. Or to put it in the political slogan of the thirties, There's no free lunch! The next question, a corollary to the main question, then becomes, Am I willing to pay what it costs?

When someone consults with an astrologer or psychologist it is usually because something in his life has gotten out-of-balance and there is pain. Frequently this pain stems from the fact that something they are bartering for is costing them too much, and in effect the astrologer will point this out and ask the client whether he/she is willing to pay such a high price. Typical is the married couple whose continued relationship becomes increasingly painful but who agree to remain together until their children have grown up. Such a bargain costs them both a lot, and sometimes a certain amount of pain cannot be avoided—only lessened. A part of the maturation process is learning to accept the consequences of the trades that we make.

In business, when an importer and an exporter discover that they have commodities to trade they usually draw up a contract under which they agree to do business. Each agrees to offer the other certain of his resources under certain specified terms and conditions. The contract may be either oral or written. As long as both parties to the contract live up to its terms and conditions, there is a free exchange of commodities between them and the business relationship remains pleasant for both. Some contracts also contain penalty clauses where if one party fails to live up to his agreement that party suffers some loss thereby. All contracts contain at least the knowledge by both parties that should one party default all bets are off and the exchange of whatever is involved ceases.

Whether we like it or not—and I've met many clients who don't want to view things in the crass terms of business—our relationship with other people involves a social contract, either implied, as in a friendship, or actually written in some instances of legal marriage. In marriage, each party to the contract promises to cleave unto the other exclusively, for better or worse, until they are parted by death. The penalty for breach of contract is divorce and loss of the resources that each has agreed to exchange with the other for the rest of their lives. Divorce is painful, but so must have been the marriage. Each partner to the marriage contract has to decide whether at some future time following, the marriage bargain they struck at the altar is too costly to continue. In deciding upon divorce one or both of the parties to the marital contract has determined that to get a divorce is less painful than to continue the relationship. Every social bargain that we strike with another person costs us something, and the later breaking of that bargain also becomes costly. Some people are good bargainers and some are not—they have to learn to bargain the hard way. And if we choose we can learn the hard way, or we can use astrology, specifically the natal chart, to first identify those areas of bargaining where we are initially weak and use care in contracting in this area of our life.

A few bad bargains, early in life, usually ending painfully, will sometimes lead the individual to conclude that he/she will make no more bargains or trades for certain resources. Examples would be a man or woman who has a bad marital experience and determines never to marry again or a person who offers love freely, is badly mistreated in the deal and concludes never to love another ever again. Thus, they put one of their valuble resources into permanent storage where it does neither themselves or anyone else any good. To put it another way, they have determined that the bartering of this resource is too costly to them.

As I pointed out before, there are inherent risks in all trades. You have to be willing to take these risks if import/export is to take place. Soon I will show you how you can identify these risks in your natal chart. Before we do this, however, there are several other factors that must be considered. These factors are associated with pride.

Not only does a series of successful import/export deals with others start to bring us what we are seeking in terms of resources that we lack, but it also brings us a certain amount of self-satisfaction and pride in ourselves. It helps to validate and improve our self-image, for we conclude that we are "okay" and take pride in our ability to bargain successfully. In a society that measures success in terms of how well we are able to bargain to get what we want, especially when the trophies of this bargain are tangible and on display for others to admire, we are said by others (and ourselves) to be "successful." This is really what Dr. Thomas A. Harris is saying in his book, *I'm Okay—You're Okay*. He is talking about that point at which we can say to ourselves, "I am a success at the import/export game, others recognize my success at this game, and I can continue to make such bargains without taking undue advantage of others or looking down upon those who are less successful bargainers than I."

Successful bargains enhance our public reputation and add to our personal pride in ourselves and our abilities. In a truly free enterprise system this import/export game as played by individuals goes on practically unchecked. Under other forms of government, restrictions and special rules are placed upon how this game is to be played. In other societies, success is measured in terms other than how well its members play the import/export game.

To be a successful trader, an individual must be willing to take social risks and overcome the fear of potential failure. Sometimes the offer of a deal or a trade will be refused at the outset, and if the offer is public enough can cost the offerer something in personal pride. The suitor who asks the young lady's hand in marriage always runs the risk of her refusal, which can cost the suitor a blow to his pride. A part of being successful as a bargainer is to learn to handle an occasional refusal of an offer to trade, to learn when to turn down an unprofitable offer from others, and especially how to compromise to get the best deal possible.

How then can astrology help us to play the import/export game to greatest advantage?

As you can see in the diagram, the first six houses of the horoscope (below the horizon line) symbolize what we have to offer in exchange for what we are seeking. The last six houses, each of which has its polar opposite house below the horizon, symbolize what we are seeking in exchange. Each polar house pair, a spectrum, represents a trade in a particular field of life.

Let's take as an example one commodity that is especially valued by most people, love. This commodity is represented by the fifth/eleventh house spectrum. The fifth house

Figure 5

represents love offered; the eleventh house represents love sought. We all need and seek love; however, to get the love of others we must be willing to offer our own love in return.

I'm sure that you have observed that some people require a lot more love than others, or, to put it another way, place a greater value on love than other commodities, just as King Midas valued gold above all else. And there are still others who have a lot of love to give to other people. Quantitative assessments in astrology are never easy to make. However, you can get a pretty good picture of how much by what Marc Edmund Jones refers to as "preponderance." The more planets in the house, the greater the emphasis and thus the greater the need as perceived by that individual. With several planets in the eleventh house, an individual perceives a stronger need for the love of others than the individual with no eleventh house planets. Love given or shared with this individual by others is held in greater esteem and value. How this individual will go about obtaining this commodity and how he/she perceives love, will be characteristic of the actual planets that tenant this house. Mars here would make the individual more aggressive in pursuit of love; Venus, on the other hand, though requiring more love, would tend to wait for it. Neptune here would contribute to the individual's perception of love as something quite spiritual and idealistic, while Saturn here might signify certain fears that must be overcome before allowing others to love him.

Now let's look at the fields each polar house pair represents.

First/Seventh House: Identity and Recognition This polarity reveals the need of the individual to establish his own identity and have it recognized and validated by others as being "okay." This is the first house. However, to do so he must be willing to give equal recognition to the identity of others and be willing to validate them as being okay too. The bargain: I'll offer you recognition and identity as a person in your own right if you'll offer me the same. Planets in these houses amplify this need.

Second/Eighth House: Property and Sex This polarity reveals the need of the individual for possessions and the physical sharing of himself with another person through sex. Money is often the commodity being exchanged. The bargain: I'll offer you something I possess for some asset you possess in exchange. Of course, the greatest physical asset we possess is our own physical body, which we give in the act of sex.

Third/Ninth House: Freedom and Wisdom Ideas and knowledge are intangible assets we possess that can be traded. That's why there are patent and copyright laws to protect ideas. In no area or our being are we freer than within our own minds. Our thinking is limited only by self-imposed limitations. The bargain: Let's exchange ideas, for the truth shall give us both greater freedom.

Fourth/Tenth House: Group Identity and Security This house polarity deals with our perception of what makes us feel secure and what makes us feel more powerful. In this area of life we are bargaining for greater power from those more powerful than we (tenth house), public standing and reputation, and in return exchanging a part of our personal security to obtain it. As in all trades it involves sacrifice; people in the public eye give up an important portion of their private lives.

Fifth/Eleventh House: The Pursuit of Happiness This polarity deals with the exchange of intangible commodities and assets like love, children, vacations, hobbies, and what we have come to call "the good life" that tend to bring us greater enjoyment and happiness. This polarity deals with our romantic desires and needs. Whereas the second/eighth house polarity deals with things physically conceived (through sexual activity), this polarity deals with things mentally conceived. The basic bargain here is, of course: Love me and I will love you. **Sixth/Twelfth House: Integration and Service**   Bargains relating to this polarity are rather elusive. It's too simplistic to reduce it to the obvious "Serve me and I will serve you; protect me and I will protect you." The type of bargain can range from simply dealing with others for the necessities of life like food and clothing to "Care for me and I will care for you," all the way to "Help me find my place in the universe and I will help you to do likewise." Here, words and communication are put to the test of reality. It can be the supplicant saying to God, "God, do this for me and I will do this for you." It can mean, "Suffer for me and I will suffer for you."

The above descriptions are not especially meant to be complete in themselves; rather they are designed to give you some of the flavor of what is being bartered and what is being bartered for. You must also keep in mind that those things we conventionally associate with each house must also be considered in any analysis of the commerce taking place.

I would like to suggest at this point that you stop your reading of this chapter temporarily and get out a pencil and paper. Forgetting totally for the moment what you know of your own horoscope, I want you to make two lists. In the first list, write down in descending order of importance to you, what you want most from your relationships with others. Things like love, sex, security, recognition, attention, money, etc. Then, in the second list carefully assess all of the things "commodities" that you have to offer to others in return for those things that you want. If you're really objective about this, the second list should be longer than the first. If your second list is shorter than the first list, then perhaps you'd better reassess your own assets. Or as the psychologists would put it you need to improve upon your own "self-image."

"Masculine" and "Feminine" Signs

At this point I am afraid that I am going to get into controversy with some of the more traditional professional astrologers who insist on the Ptolemaic classification of the signs as being alternatively masculine and feminine and also with those who insist on using the Ptolemaic system for astrological birth control and conception determinations. As I see it, the sign polarities do fit into a symmetrical system, but not in the traditional sense. This symmetrical system, as I see it, is shown in the table below.

Positive and Negative Signs in the Sign Polarities

Positive Sign	Negative Sign
Aries	Libra
Scorpio	Taurus
Sagittarius	Gemini
Capricorn	Cancer
Leo	Aquarius
Virgo	Pisces

I think it will be clear to those who know the personality characteristics associated with each of the signs that the six positive signs are the most aggressive members of each of the pairs and the six negative signs, the more receptive in each case. Is there any question in your mind that this is so? Then why continue to use the old Ptolemaic classification? The words "masculine" and "feminine" are misnomers and lead one to attribute characteristics to a sign that it really does not possess. Do you realy think that Scorpio, for example, is "feminine?" Or, Capricorn?

In our astrological vocabularies, let's start to substitute the words "active" and "passive" or "positive" and "negative" (I prefer the former) for "masculine" and "feminine."

Applying this Theory to Eclipses

Assuming that at this point you are at least willing to accept this idea as a working hypothesis, let us now proceed to investigate how it might apply to the delineation of the effect of eclipses upon the natal horoscope and thus upon a progressed yearly forecast.

Turn now to your own natal horoscope, which is undoubtedly the horoscope which you know the best, and test these ideas out for yourself. I am going to suggest a few rules here for you to follow in delineating eclipse effects upon it.

Recall first that we've already pointed out that houses one through six represent your need to "export," to trade resources that you have and houses seven through twelve

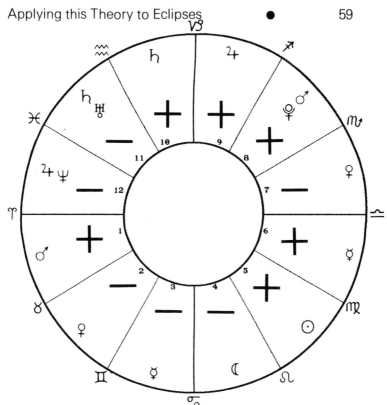

Figure 6: A Proposed System of Polar Opposite Signs

represent your need to "import," to trade for those things that you lack and need to become a whole person. How aggressively you pursue these needs will depend upon whether you have an active or passive sign on the cusp of this house.

The occurrence of an eclipse in a particular house brings the particular need that is related to this house to the foreground of your attention. The need becomes emphasized and a crisis may develop in regard to this house if you have problems in this area of your life that are not being adequately attended to.

If the eclipse is also conjunct a particular natal planet (orb ±5°) then this need will tend to be felt more strongly. If the eclipse is opposed to a particular natal planet (orb ±5°) then this need will still be felt more strongly, but in addition it is a signal that the energies from the opposing house must be used in the solution of problems related to the house that the eclipse is in. For example, if the eclipse is in the fifth house and opposed to a planet in the eleventh house, this symbolically suggests that if you really want to share your love with another, you must be willing to let the other person love you as much in return. Simple to say; sometimes difficult to do!

In most cases, the lunar eclipse, when it occurs, will be in the house opposing the house in which the solar eclipse occurs. In the above example, this suggests (even without a planet opposing the eclipse position) that feeling a need to share your love you must test the ability of the other person to share his/her love with you. The house in which the accompanying lunar eclipse occurs is always the house in which some testing must occur, especially in view of the fact that testing preceeds action and that the next solar eclipse will usually fall in this house six months later. If the testing is done properly under the lunar eclipse emphasis, then when the next solar eclipse occurs in this house you are better prepared to deal with it. The solar eclipse produces less shock and is thus less traumatic.

Usually the solar-lunar pair occurs in the same house polarity. When it is across the line of the sign and not in the same house polarity it is a period of preparation for the transition of house-pair emphasis from one polarity into the next, the Moon preparing the way for this transition. ·

The house in which the solar eclipse occurs is an area of life in which there is a need to expand the space we occupy, at the physical, emotional, mental or spiritual level, depending upon which element (earth, water, air or fire) the eclipse occupies by sign, to aggressively pursue each expansion if in a positive sign, to let it happen if in a negative sign.

The house in which the accompanying lunar eclipse (or appulse) occurs is the area of life in which you should be preparing for the next solar eclipse.

Every well-run company or organization periodically goes through certain review processes to check upon the efficiency of various departments within the company and make sure that they are running at maximum efficiency, doing the job that they are supposed to accomplish and not placing excessive demands upon the resources of the company. Note that it is only the successive series of eclipses that runs "backwards" through the zodiac. Everything else runs forward (counterclockwise) around the circle of the zodiac.

Eclipses emphasize the review process that must take place in our lives. Whether you like it or not, eclipses test you out on how well you are doing with respect to each house in your horoscope. They force you to review matters in terms of the house in which the solar eclipse has fallen. They give you an opportunity to set your house in order and get your act together in terms of this particular area of life. The spotlight is thrown upon this house during the period of effect of the eclipse, and all of those things in this house that have been neglected or hidden come in for a good house cleaning. Eclipses are scorpionic in effect. They force you to separate what is of value from the junk and then force you to unload the junk. They are purgative in their effect upon your life. If you have a clean house, the effect of the eclipse is less traumatic. The preceding lunar eclipse in this house is a warning that the house will shortly be inspected. It signals an opportunity to do some housecleaning before the inspector gets there.

When we get to the chapter on rectification of the chart and examine the horoscope of the United States as an example, this principle will, I think, be adequately demonstrated.

Keeping these factors in mind, the next question is, how long does this eclipse emphasis last? In the next chapter I will attempt to answer this question.

7 ● Duration of Effect

The question of how long a solar or lunar eclipse influences human behavior has been debated since the earliest days of astrology. No one has yet provided us with a definitive answer to this question. Until a lot more research has been done, perhaps the best we can do is to rely on our own observations. In this chapter I will share my own observations with you.

The earliest astrologers or astrologer-priests did not use a circular chart with twelve houses as we do today. It was the Greek scientist-astrologer Ptolemy who codified and organized the ancient knowledge at his disposal at that time into our modern system. While Ptolemy's work was of great benefit in advancing the study of astrology, his system of codification was not without a number of deficiencies.

In his codification of astrology Ptolemy made many statements that have never been tested scientifically. Too many astrologers for far too long have been content to blindly follow Ptolemy's rules without testing them in the light of present knowledge.

A blatant example of this is astrology's blind acceptance of Ptolemy's rule for the duration of effect of eclipses. Ptolemy stated that the duration of effect of a solar eclipse lasts as long in years (some say months) as the eclipse actually lasts in minutes, from the time it first commences until the time it passes. Since the duration of a solar eclipse can be as long as 7.5 minutes for totality (average about 3 minutes), eclipse effects must persist for over a decade if one considers the time from commencement to ending of the eclipse. Ptolemy asserts that the effect of a lunar eclipse lasts as long in months as the eclipse lasts in minutes.

Since Ptolemy's time other rules have crept into eclipse interpretation. For example, it has been said that when transiting Mars comes into conjunction with the last eclipse point or a recent eclipse point, it tends to emphasize and bring to the foreground whatever it is that the eclipse has indicated or presaged. This is a nice theory, but it has never been tested for accuracy. On the surface, this rule has some plausibility because we know that Mars transits do have a way of making things happen in our lives that can be disruptive. However, we must also remember that such a transit occurs simultaneously in the horoscope of every living being on this Earth at the same instant, albeit in different houses, which implies that every living being should experience some crisis in his life at precisely the same moment. To me, this does not fit with observable facts. When we as astrologers make such pronouncements that fly in the face of logic, we injure the cause of acceptance of astrology by the public.

From time to time I keep hearing another rule from various sources that states that the eclipse effect persists until the eclipse point is transited by Saturn. Saturn takes almost twenty-nine years to complete one transit of the zodiac. This implies that there will be cases when an eclipse occurs just behind Saturn's current position in the zodiac and the eclipse effect will linger for almost twenty-nine years. This rule is harder to disprove, for we have no accurate means of assessing just how long the effect of an eclipse persists. Assuming that the effect of an eclipse can be a traumatic experience for us at times, and considering the basic tenet of astrology that the effect of the birth moment persists for an entire lifetime (also certainly a traumatic experience for the emerging infant), and further considering that psychologists tell us that early traumatic childhood experiences can influence the behavior for an entire lifetime, it is difficult to assess the validity of this rule. It may well be correct.

Considering that eclipses occur about six lunar months apart, we know that the Moon will make five to six transits of the eclipse point before the next eclipse occurs. We also know that the Moon is often the timer of events in our lives. Considering the fact that the Moon's conjunction with an eclipse point also occurs simultaneously in the lives of every living human being, can we assume that the Moon too brings our attention to what the eclipse point has to tell us in our particular horoscope? Perhaps.

There are a lot of open questions here that I cannot answer. Only you can decide the validity of these rules based upon your own experience. I find it most interesting that the Mars rule, the Saturn rule and the Moon rule cannot be traced back to any one particular astrological observer. Rather, they seem to be a part of the mythology of astrology that many have come to accept without question and without testing. In my own experience, these rules do not apply. Perhaps I am less sensitive to such experiences than others who have preceeded me. I do not think so. By watching where and for how long each eclipse effect persists in your own life, you can answer this question for yourself.

You may ask at this point, If you throw out all of the previous rules governing the duration of effect of eclipses, what rule do you put in its place? Based upon my observations of my own life and the lives of my clients, the rule that I follow is simply this: *The effect of an eclipse persists from the time that it occurs until the time of occurrence of the next eclipse, solar to solar, lunar to lunar.* This may not be true, but for me it appears to work, and those for whom I do chart delineations respond positively to this rule. As a scientist, I should really call it a hypothesis because I am unable to prove it scientifically, except in terms of my own personal observation.

I hope you will test and evaluate this hypothesis in the light of your personal experience before either accepting or rejecting it and I would appreciate any observations or comments in support or rejection of this hypothesis.

I see very little evidence to support the notion that eclipses have any effect prior to their occurence, as some writers suggest. On the other hand, I've observed immediate effects of eclipses in the lives of individuals in terms of the house location of the eclipse, within just a few days of occurrence.

I recall vividly a personal experience where within five days following an eclipse in my second house I was forced to deal with a crisis involving the investment of money received from the sale of my home. On another occasion, within only two days of an eclipse in my eleventh house, I was faced with the death of a close friend. Many other experiences related to me by friends and clients lead me to believe that at least the intensity of the eclipse effect makes itself known shortly after the eclipse occurs and in relation to the house in the horoscope in which the eclipse occurs. While the effects may "tail out" over a longer period, it does not take long to identify the house crisis associated with an eclipse once it has occurred, especially when the eclipse occurs in conjunction with a natal planetary position in the natal horoscope, and most especially when it is in conjunction with the natal position of the Sun or Moon. In a later chapter I will present some actual case studies to demonstrate this effect.

Eclipses in Counseling

It is not uncommon for a practicing professional astrologer to set up an appointment with a new client to discuss the client's problems that seem most pressing at the moment. In a brief phone conversation, it is not always easy to discern this problem or problems. However, in preparing the natal chart prior to the consultation and in noting where the last solar eclipse has occurred in the natal horoscope, I find that almost invariably the problems that the client faces are those associated with the house in his/her chart in which the last solar eclipse has occurred. And when this eclipse is conjunct (± 5 °) a natal point in the chart, the problem that the client faces is of major proportions.

Even when the problem presented falls naturally in another house of the client's chart, the root cause of the problem can invariably be traced to the house in which the last solar eclipse occurred. In making this statement, I realize that I am doing exactly what I have accused Ptolemy of doing, making a blanket statement without supporting scientific evidence. In defense I can only say that my own observations tend to support my contention.

Every practising astrologer deals with the repeat client who returns, year after year, to have an astrological forecast done for the coming year. I can only share my personal experience with you in saying that, by considering the transits to natal positions in the chart and taking into account the houses in which eclipses will occur during that year, I find that I can do a very satisfactory forecast for the client. This is not to say that progressions are not important, especially the positions of the progressed Sun, Moon and ascendant; however, the progressed aspects and positions merely serve to reinforce the information that the eclipse positions and transits already presage for the client.

I think that you will also discover that if you ask your subject or client what it is that is currently demanding more of his/her time and attention than usual, you will invariably be able to retrace this concern to the house in which the last solar eclipse occurred. Give it a try and prove it for yourself. Once you have done so, I think you will be convinced, as I have been, that to do a forecast without considering the position of the eclipses that will occur during that year only provides you with incomplete information. Eclipse positions, even more so than a solar return chart, give you a primary key to the problems your client must face and deal with during the coming year.

I leave this question of how long the eclipse effect lasts to your own observations. If your observations agree with my own, you will be convinced that for practical purposes the emphatic eclipse effect lasts from the time of occurrence of that eclipse until the time of occurrence of the next like eclipse, finding expression in terms of the house in which this eclipse has occurred.

8 ● The Prenatal Eclipse

My own research and the observations of others who are interested in eclipse phenomena lead me to believe that we ought
to pay careful attention to the house in the horoscope in which
the last solar eclipse occurred prior to birth. This prenatal
eclipse point can easily be determined from an ephemeris or
from the eclipse tables in the appendix to this book. The date
of the eclipse will always be within six lunar months of the
birthdate and usually in the house occupied by the Moon's
north or south node in the natal chart.

Once you have located and identified this point in your
natal chart, watch the correspondence between conjunctions
of transiting planets with this point and events that occur in
your life. I am convinced that this prenatal eclipse point
should be treated in the same way as all of the planetary positions in your natal chart, and it should also be watched for
transits to this point in the same manner you watch for transits
to the natal planetary positions in your chart.

Just as the current eclipse position emphasizes matters in your life that are connected with the house in which it occurs, the house in which the prenatal eclipse occurred seems to be continually emphasized throughout the life of the individual, even though it might not contain natal planets or other astrological factors that would bring it into prominence. I have, for example, observed a number of cases in which the individuals concerned were deeply involved in the teaching or rearing of children, where children continued to play a prominent role and receive great emphasis in their lives, and yet the fifth house in the chart was unoccupied and unemphasized. The only logical reason for this emphasis in these charts was that the prenatal eclipse had occurred in the fifth house.

In other charts that I have observed, I have found planets that were strong and heavily emphasized in the life of the individual that, by normal rules of power assessment, were not brought into prominence in the chart because of planetary pattern, chart rulership or any of the other normally recognized rules of power emphasis. What then proved to be the answer? It was merely that the emphasized planet was either conjunct or opposed ($\pm 5°$) to the position of that prenatal eclipse point.

I would therefore recommend that you now take a moment to determine the position of the prenatal eclipse point in your own natal chart. In which house did this eclipse fall? Do you feel that the affairs related to this house are of unusual importance and emphasis in your life? Is this prenatal eclipse point either conjunct or opposite the position of any of your natal planets? If so, do you feel that this planet, the transits that it makes to other planets, or the transits made by other planets to this point, receive powerful emphasis in what they symbolize in your life? If your answer is "yes" to any of these questions, then I am sure I do not need to convince you any further.

To express this idea in a different manner, the house in which your prenatal eclipse occurred is an area of your life that needs to be expanded, an area in which you feel that you need a lot of space to expand and grow. The sign on the cusp of this house and the element in which it is located indicate on which level this expansion ought to take place. If, for example, the prenatal eclipse is in the fifth house, which has an air sign on its cusp, then the indication is that expansion of the creative principle on the intellectual-mental level is called for. This is an indication of high mental creativity. If, on the other hand, an earth sign occupies the fifth house cusp, then the creative principle needs expression on the physical level and one would therefore be more inclined to create new children.

The main idea here is to give yourself considerable opportunity for expansion of yourself in the area of life in which the prenatal eclipse occurred and on the level (physical, mental, emotional, spiritual) indicated by the sign on the cusp of this house. If the prenatal eclipse is conjunct a planet in this house, then the indication is that the energy represented by the planet ought to be used to its fullest capacity in this expansion process. If the prenatal eclipse is opposed to some planet in the opposite house, then the indication is that the affairs of that house and the energy represented by that planet must be integrated in the process of expanding affairs related to the house in which the prenatal eclipse occurred.

The Solar Eclipse Return

The above rules appear to apply only to the prenatal solar eclipse; I have not been able to observe a similar effect for its corresponding lunar eclipse if it has one.

In previous chapters I have pointed out that when a solar eclipse occurs in conjunction with the position of the natal Sun and Moon it is usually symbolic of some major event or happening in the life of the individual. Often these events are of great importance and can be turning points in that person's life. Eclipses conjunct natal Sun or Moon are more emphatic in their effect than eclipses conjunct other natal points. To the Sun and Moon we must now add a third point of great emphasis, the position of the prenatal solar eclipse. The return of the solar eclipse to the prenatal eclipse point ($\pm 5°$ of orb maximum) will occur every eighteen years and usually signals some crisis in the person's life of major importance.

I think the reason why previous writers on this subject have failed to notice this point is that the first two prenatal eclipse returns occur at ages eighteen and thirty-six. Both of these ages are key years in the life cycle for other reasons. Thus the prenatal eclipse return with its symbolic indication of emphasis and crisis has been masked. Age thirty-six, for example,

is a key year (often a traumatic one) in everyone's life, symbolized by the formation of squares by Saturn and the progressed Moon to their natal positions in the horoscope. At this
same time the Moon's nodes have also returned to their natal
positions. These planetary factors set you up for the return of
the prenatal eclipse and with its occurrence the fireworks
usually start. Both Marc Robertson in *The Transit of Saturn*,
and Gail Sheehy in *Passages* do a fine job of describing this
crisis time, so I will not attempt to elaborate on it further except to say that the prenatal eclipse return figures prominently
in the astrological symbolism for this age.

Age eighteen signals the first prenatal eclipse return and we
know this is a very trying age in the life of every young person.
In the United States he or she has just graduated from high
school and has come to a very important fork in the road of
life. The young person has a number of options open, and the
question becomes which road to follow. Perhaps this has
puzzled you in terms of the planetary cycles as it once puzzled
me. At age eighteen Saturn is trine its natal position—so that
won't explain it. Only Jupiter is in hard aspect (opposed) to its
natal position, along with a Mars return during this year.
These aspects do not denote in the necessary emphatic terms
the crisis that usually occurs here. What, then, is the answer?
The only one that I can find that satisfies me is, of course, the
first prenatal eclipse return. It clearly symbolizes the crisis that
occurs in a very sensitive area of the person's life (which the
prenatal eclipse has previously sensitized by its position in the
natal chart).

Both of these occasions give us, as astrologers, an ideal opportunity to observe and verify what we already understand
about eclipses. The symbolic crisis that occurs at these ages
often involves some sort of break with tradition and/or the
way the individual has been doing things in the past. It is a
time of questioning the old ways and trying out new ones. To
this extent eclipses are uranian in their basic nature; however,
unlike Uranus which tends to force such issues, the eclipse only presents the opportunity for change without forcing.

Many astrologers do not pay much attention to quintile and
biquintile aspects in the horoscope. I do because I believe that
they too offer us alternative opportunities for expression when
we get tired of sextiles. When do quintiles begin to come into
prominence in our charts and lives? After about age thirty-six,

the second prenatal eclipse return. It is at about this age that many people first begin to realize that life offers them alternatives: alternative life styles, alternative ways of making a living, alternative ways of thinking. The characteristics of a generation (symbolized by Pluto) do not seem to come to full fruition until the bulk of that generation has had its second prenatal eclipse return at age thirty-six.

I recommend very strongly that you keep your own personal eclipse log. In keeping this log, watch especially those years at which you reach the ages of eighteen, thirty-six, fifty-four, seventy-two and ninety, the years of the prenatal eclipse returns. Also watch the years in which you reach nine, twenty-seven, forty-five, sixty-three and eighty-one. These are the years when there will be an eclipse that opposes your prenatal eclipse point. Carefully record your observations. As you review this log from time to time, try to see how you felt a need to "expand your space" at these times.

Your personal eclipse log should include the following information about your prenatal solar eclipse: date, sign position, house position, conjunct planet(s), opposed planet(s), number of days prior to birth, planetary ruler, conjunct fixed stars, planets conjunct horizon.

While we are on the subject of returns I want to draw your attention to two other returns that also ought to be watched. This will be a very individualized phenomenon peculiar to your own natal chart. Watch the returns to the position where a solar eclipse occurs conjunct the position of your natal Sun and natal Moon. These eclipses will be of great importance in your life because they signal and symbolize a crisis involving one of the luminaries, especially when this occurs between the ages of twenty-one and sixty. Such eclipses often signal important turning points in the life of the individual or at least the opportunity to strike off in some new direction. They should be interpreted in terms of some crisis associated with the house location of the luminary.

9 ● Eclipses in Rectification

A good general understanding of eclipses and their effects in the delineation of a natal chart is just one of the many advantages to the practicing astrologer that can come from studying the eclipses. Eclipses also provide us with a very useful and powerful tool in the rectification of charts of uncertain or unknown birthtime. In this chapter I will show you how to use eclipses in rectification, and we will use this tool to examine two possible horoscopes for the United States to see if we can draw some conclusion as to which of the two charts is the most accurate.

It's important to point out right away that you cannot rectify a chart using only eclipses. Eclipses provide us with one technique that must be used with others to do a proper job of rectification. I use eclipses as the first step in the process. There are other much more precise steps that you must follow once you have placed the eclipse in the proper house. These you can find in any of the various books on rectification available. However, eclipses will get you started and help you to narrow down the choice of possible midheavens and ascendants to at most two possibilities. When you have no idea at all what time of day the subject was born, this can be a big first step. Here's how you do it.

Let us assume for the moment that it is your own horoscope that you are trying to rectify. As pointed out previously, our lives move from crisis to crisis. There is always some house in the horoscope that is "in review" and emphasized at any time you examine the situation. You must first determine where the immediate crisis is in your life at the moment.

Next, determine the position of the last *solar* eclipse that has occurred by its sign and degree location in the zodiac.

Finally, place this location right in the middle of the house that by symbolism is most closely associated with the current crisis in your life. This will take some careful thought, because you may be faced with several possible houses in which to place the eclipse position. Perhaps this is best illustrated using several examples.

Let us assume that the most important problem in your life at the moment is a financial crisis. This would lead you to assume that the eclipse must be in either the second or eighth house (see chapter 6). Is the problem one of what to do with money you already have? This would make it a second house crisis. Or is the problem, Where am I going to get more money in order to pay all of my current bills? This would make it an eighth house crisis. The general principle is that if you are concerned with a problem of what to do with something you already have, you are dealing with some house below the horizon line (houses one through six). If your principal concern is in getting something that you do not already possess, then the problem lies in a house above the horizon (houses seven through twelve).

If for example, you are looking for someone to give your love to, this is a fifth house matter. If you are looking for someone to love you, then we are probably dealing with an eleventh house matter. You've got to think things through very carefully and analyze the situation as objectively as possible. Are you really looking for someone to *love*, or is it more a matter of finding someone you can *serve*, which would place the emphasis in the sixth house? Is it really love you are seeking, or is it more a question of finding a good sex partner, which would put the emphasis likely in the second house? For this method to work, you've got to be really analytical and truthful with yourself, or get your client to the point where he/she is comfortable enough with you to be truthful and analyze his/her feelings. This cannot be a superficial judgement; it must be thought through very carefully.

Let's take another example. Suppose you are dealing with a frequently asked question these days, Should I divorce my spouse? And suppose you do not have a correct birthtime for the person. How would you place the eclipse position in the horosocope? The problem is to get at the underlying motivation for wanting the divorce in the first place. Where does the real problem lie by house position?

Is the problem sexual incompatibility (eighth house)? a desire for greater freedom (ninth house)? an illicit love affair (twelfth house)? financial reasons (eighth house)? or a conflict of personalities (seventh house)? Does your client want the divorce (houses seven through twelve), or does your client's spouse want the divorce? (houses one through six).

This may sound like a pretty good method for rectifying a chart, but you've got to be aware of certain pitfalls in this process. You must ask yourself whether the crisis is really symbolized by the eclipse, or is it perhaps signified instead by a transit of one of the middle or outer planets to a natal planet in the house associated with the crisis? We're not always faced with one crisis at a time, you know!

I prefer to do such rectifications at a time in the person's life when there are not a lot of other complicating factors in the horoscope. However, this is not always possible in the situation you are dealing with. For example, I do not like to do such rectifications under the conjunction of an eclipse with the position of the natal Sun. In the first place, this is always a time of great stress on the subject, a time when he/she is least able to tell where the problem really lies. The subject tends to feel this stress in every area of his/her life. Then, too, at this time you are dealing with an ego crisis which tends to obscure the real roots of the crisis. The client usually feels like he/she is going off in twelve different directions at once and cannot possibly cope with his/her life.

I also do not like to do such rectifications under the influence of an eclipse that is conjunct the position of the natal

Moon. At this time the subject is usually under great emotional stress and unable to sort out where the real problem lies.

I much prefer to do such rectifications based upon eclipses that occur at relatively quiet periods of the person's life when they are able to reflect back rationally and objectively on past situations. My preference is for using eclipse positions that are neither conjunct nor opposed to a natal planetary position in the chart.

Eclipses also provide us with golden opportunities to test the validity of charts, where there appear to be two or more well-established but conflicting birth times given, or, conversely, to test the validity of the principles I have outlined in this book regarding eclipses.

The Chart of the USA

As you are probably well aware, several horoscopes that have been proposed as the correct horoscope for the United States of America. How do you decide which to accept? Eclipse positions provide us with the key.

Charts 1 and 2 are two horoscopes that have been proposed for the United States. Chart 1 (on page 76) is the horoscope that a majority of astrologers have come to recognize as the correct one, with 7° Gemini 35' in the ascendant and 13° Aquarius 57' at the midheaven. Chart 2 (on page 77) is the contender, with an ascendant of 13° Libra 32' and a midheaven of 15° Cancer 37'. The unique feature of this second chart is the preponderance of planets (six) in the ninth house. Which is correct?

Chart 1 uses what is purportedly the time the Declaration of Independence was signed—7:14:55 GMT, July 4, 1776, Philadelphia, Pennsylvania. Chart 2 uses 12:15 PM, July 4, 1776, Philadelphia, Pennsylvania, based upon the Congressional Record for July 4, 1776, which states:

> "Agreeable to the order of the day, the Congress resolved itself into a committee of the whole, to take into further consideration the Declaration and after some time the President resumed his chair, and Mr. Harrison reported that the Committee had agreed to a Declaration that they desired to report.... At a little past meridian, on the Fourth of July, 1776, a unanimous vote of the thirteen colonies was given in favor of declaring themselves free and independent states."

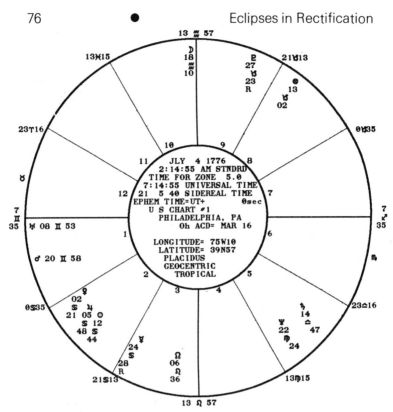

Chart 1: The United States of America

Now, which chart shall we use? Both seem well supported
by authorities, historical and astrological. A careful examina-
tion of these two charts reveals enough differences between
them to pose a problem. The second chart contains a yod, with
the Moon in focal position, and the composition of the grand
air trine also changes. One can I think, make a good case for
either chart on the basis of its natal interpretation, but which
of the two will stand up under the acid test when we begin to
use it in forecasting? Which chart most clearly demonstrates
the crisis situations that we find in the headlines of our current
newspapers? Based on my own analysis, I believe it is chart 1
with Gemini rising, but I leave the ultimate decision to you.
Let's look at the facts.

The 1976 presidential election was held on Tuesday,
November 2. On October 23, 1976, just prior to the election,
we had a total solar eclipse at 0° Scorpio 4′. In chart 1 this
would place the eclipse in the sixth house. In chart 2 it would

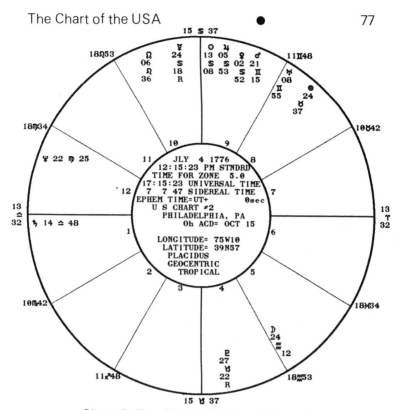

Chart 2: The United States of America

fall in the first house, neither opposed nor conjunct any natal planetary positions—a good opportunity to make an objective evaluation. In their evaluations of this election and the factors that most influenced the voting public, both *Time* and *Newsweek* judged the major issue to be "jobs." Jobs, the service we give to others, is a sixth house matter (chart 1). The labor unions (sixth house) also figured prominently in the outcome. However, it was indeed the people of the nation, though a minority of them, that made their voice heard (first house in chart 2). The argument is not compelling but I think chart 1 is favored. With Saturn in the first house, (Saturn too symbolizing the productive use of time—labor) you can create an interesting case for chart 2 as well.

On November 3, 1975, there was a partial solar eclipse at 10° Scorpio 28′, which places it in the sixth house of chart 1 and the first house of chart 2. Hardly had this eclipse occurred when suddenly, according to the headlines, the nation was faced with a health crisis, the skyrocketing cost of medical malpractice insurance. A medical crisis (sixth house)! President Ford was also faced with the decision of whether to proceed with production of the influenza vaccine to prevent a possible epidemic. Clearly a sixth house matter: the public health.

From 1975 through 1977 there have been three solar eclipses in the twelfth house of chart 1. With so many problems facing our nation, where did Congress spend the bulk of its time, energy and attention? On investigations of the FBI, CIA, NSA and other undercover and covert organizations and activities—twelfth house matters.

During this same period we saw a number of powerful representatives and senators toppled from their positions of power and prominence when the door to their closet of secret allegiances and activities was thrown open to the public view under the influence of twelfth house eclipses, as is so often the case. At this writing, the United States remains under the influence of a twelfth house eclipse that occurred on April 18, 1977, at 28° Aries. We find Congress investigating itself again for undercover payoffs from the South Korean Government. Bribery is involved. We are faced with a mounting balance-of-payments deficit. Medicare is an issue, as well as reform of our welfare system. Labor union pension systems are under investigation. There is discussion of extending the retirement age from sixty-five to seventy. We are still slaughtering cattle that have been contaminated with insecticides. The legalization of Laetrile and its possible dangerous side effects is being carefully studied all over the nation. All of these are twelfth house matters.

When we examine chart 2 for the position of this latest eclipse we discover that it occurred in house seven. While it is true that Secretary of State Vance is busily engaged in diplomatic activites in the Middle East, a seventh house matter, it does not seem to me that his activities have the urgency that other matters seem to have.

On April 4, 1977, there was a partial lunar eclipse at 14° Libra that was conjunct the US's natal Saturn at 14° Libra 48'. In chart 2 this would also have occurred conjunct the ascendant. You will recall that lunar eclipses have a way of forcing us to test out our past experiences (in the house where they occur) in the light of their present-day continuing applicability and that they have a way of foreshadowing events to come when the next solar eclipse occurs in this house.

In the July 1977 edition of *The Mercury Hour*, Ray Merriman gives us some good insights into the interpretation of eclipses as they occur in close conjunction to a natal planetary position. He says of Saturn, "Changes are demanded in one's roots and foundations, the nature of what one is striving for in life, one's objectives." Eclipses conjunct Saturn present a challenge to the basic integrity and structure of the organism, be it an individual or a nation. It is interesting to note that just following this eclipse the TV series *Roots* had its unprecedented success with the American viewing audience, which would I think perhaps favor chart 2. However, in chart 1 this lunar eclipse occurred in the fifth house, which deals with the way in which we Americans entertain ourselves, so this evidence is inconclusive.

In writing of eclipses conjunct the ascendant/descendant, Merriman concludes that, "Changes are required in one's ego structure and relationship to the environment, [learning] to live in harmony with the environment and those who make up this reality....Somebody tries to control your life." That America, with its dependency on other nations for its energy needs, is not in control of its own destiny , seems rather obvious. We are undergoing some changes in our ego-structure as a nation. However, this did not suddenly occur in April 1977. It has been happening for several years.

On the other hand, in chart 1, this lunar eclipse occurred in the fifth house and we are seeing a spectacular revival in many facets of our entertainment industry. Hollywood is regaining its former status as more and more movie companies return there to do their filming. The nostalgia trend is "in." *Star Wars* has just broken all records for movie box office receipts. With the current twelfth house solar eclipse emphasis, industry is again learning that to be successful it must faithfully serve the needs of the public. Neptune's current transit through the third house in chart 2 also suggests this possibility, but I submit not as strongly. Its transit through house seven in chart 1 (if indeed this is the correct chart) suggests that perhaps we are expecting too much, being too idealistic, in our current dealings with other nations.

The foregoing examples, I think, show the difficulty in making a determination of which chart is correct and in which chart the current and past eclipse positions rightfully belong. The choice is not an easy one.

Let's put both of these charts to another test as we continue to observe them over the coming months and years directly ahead of us.

If chart 1 is the correct chart, over the next two years we ought to be able to observe certain crises in fifth house matters until August of 1979. 1979 through 1981 may well signal a relinquishment of our national power to other nations. The eclipse of August 10, 1980 in opposition to our tenth house Moon will really put both of these charts to the test. Here we have a very close opposition to the Moon, a challenge to our power as a nation and our national reputation and especially to the Presidency.

If on the other hand, chart 2 is the correct one, then over the next few years the real challenge will be to the population of the US, our personality as a nation and under the eclipse of August 10, 1980 our creativity as a nation in altering our aims and objectives, especially as they relate to knowing which other nations are really our friends. This eclipse will, in any case, energize our grand air trine in terms of the houses occupied by the other planets that compose it, and, if chart 2 is correct, the yod whose focal point is the Moon. We face exciting times ahead, as well as a golden opportunity to put the eclipse emphasis in the horoscope in its proper perspective.

If Merriman is correct, then under the opposition of the eclipse of the Moon in 1980 we must face: "Changes...demanded in [our] emotional makeup [as a nation], and in regards to all of [our] important relationships in life, and also in regards to [our] public image."

Taking a longer view, in the year 1984, there will be a solar eclipse directly upon the chart 1 ascendant at 9° Gemini and the natal position of Uranus. This should provide us with enough insight to determine which chart is correct.

Although I advise you to stick to current events as much as possible in doing these rectifications because you usually have many more immediate details to work with, it is certainly possible to work with historical events. The problem in working with historical events, such as a wedding in doing a personal chart, is that the real facts of the situation often get lost as time passes and we tend to remember only the good things about such events (if it was a happy event) or to forget much of the detail if the event was tragic or traumatic.

Nevertheless, let's subject both of our US charts to a historical perspective. I have selected for this event the attack on Pearl Harbor on December 7, 1941. On September 21, 1941, there occurred a total eclipse of the Sun at the north node of the Moon at 28° Virgo in Saros series 16 (see appendix). This series is under the influence of its first eclipse at 6° Pisces, and we know that Pisces, with its ruler Neptune, is, among other things, associated with deceit. Also on September 5th it had an accompanying partial lunar eclipse at 13° Pisces.

In chart 1 the solar eclipse falls into the fifth house with the lunar eclipse right on the cusp of the eleventh. In chart 2, the solar eclipse falls into the twelfth house (the natural house of Pisces and Neptune) with the lunar eclipse in the fifth. In both cases the solar eclipse falls between the natal Neptune and Saturn, though 5° away from their midpoint. And none of these eclipses were within the orb of a conjunction or opposition to any natal position in either chart.

Interestingly, Neptune is usually considered to rule naval fleets and both Neptune and Saturn, harbors. Some observers also credit Neptune as the ruler of pearls.

You may have already jumped to the conclusion that chart 2 must be the correct one because, with the solar eclipse occurring in its twelfth house, it best describes the crisis. Neptune rules fleets, the twelfth house is the house of undercover activity, secret enemies and treachery. You may be right. But I think I can make an equally good case for the fifth house in chart 1 as well. I like this example because it so nicely illustrates why I mistrust historical events.

In the first place, the fifth house symbolizes ambassadors and at the time of the Pearl Harbor attack the Japanese ambassadors were negotiating in the US. The Japanese under Admiral Yamamoto clearly recognized that an attack on Pearl Harbor would be a highly "speculative" (fifth house) venture at best. Japan is generally considered to be a Libra nation and in chart 2 (with 13° of Libra in the twelfth house) you've got to be fair and at least ask, Who was deceiving whom? Were the Japanese deceiving themselves?

But let's return to chart 1. In mundane horoscopes the fifth house represents the morality of a nation, public sorrow and the youth of that nation. Certainly, the attack on Pearl Harbor was an event of great national sorrow. If the fifth house represents the public morality of the US, then the eleventh

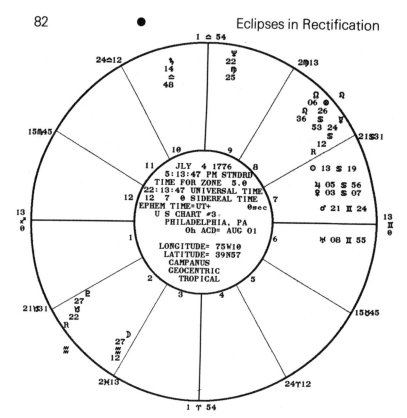

Chart 3: The United States of America

house represents the morality of our adversaries (Japan) and we find the lunar eclipse on the cusp of this house where most authorities would agree it very strongly influences that house. Need I also point out that the eleventh also deals with our international relationships (friendships) with other countries as well as treaties and alliances (both potential and actual) with them?

In chart 1 we are dealing with the fifth/eleventh house axis, what the US (fifth house) was willing to give during the ambassadorial negotiations and what Japan (eleventh house) was willing to give in return.

Or was the real crisis under this solar eclipse emphasis to the youth of our nation, to test their mettle in the face of a crisis? Certainly, American youth rose to this challenge, many of them sacrificing their lives. Now having the benefit of about thirty-five years of hindsight, what do you think the real challenge was to the United States under this crisis? Your answer will influence whether you accept chart 1 or chart 2 as being the correct one for the United States.

We sometimes jump to conclusions in doing astrological delineations, and it is not always the most obvious conclusion that is the correct one. A careful study of some of the less obvious alternatives will often yield interesting information, too.

Just to give you some practice with this technique, I have included a third chart for the United States, chart 3, proposed by Dane Rudhyar for about 5:00 PM on July 4, 1776, when, according to some reports, the Declaration was actually signed. The house cusps are calculated according to the Campanus system. Perhaps this chart is, after all, the correct one. I leave this to you to decide.

To aid you in this study, I suggest you keep your own record and notes as you observe the effects of eclipses over the next few years upon the various US charts proposed. Note especially how you view the crises that face our nation, the news that makes the daily headlines of our newspapers and judge for yourself which chart has the greatest potential for forecasting future crises.

10 ● Eclipses and Health

What are the implications of eclipses for medicine and health?

Let us first put aside as pure mythology the ancient idea that those born at the time of a total solar eclipse are either born dead or destined to rule. There is little evidence to support this, nor does there seem to be any compelling evidence to support the hypothesis that an eclipse in the eighth house signifies surgery or death. What then does the eclipse signify in a medical chart?

Elvis Presley

Let us look at one example, the natal horoscope (chart 4) of Elvis Presley, who died recently. Elvis was born in Tupelo, Mississippi (88°W43′, 34°N16′) on January 8, 1935, at 12:20 PM CST. In the appendix, we find that his pre-natal solar eclipse was at 14° Capricorn, at the north node, a partial eclipse, in Saros series 9. It occurred just three days prior to his birth, which means that it occurred conjunct his natal Sun (orb = 3°). On January 19, just following his birth, there was a total lunar eclipse at 29° Cancer in his fourth house. The solar eclipse was in his ninth house. Referring to chapter 4, we discover that Saros series 9 currently had two series going and that this solar eclipse was the last solar eclipse in the older series that was ruled by 17° of Leo, which is exactly on the cusp of Elvis' fifth house (Placidean house system). In his horoscope let us here note for future reference that his Sun (his basic vitality) is square both Mars in Libra in his sixth (health) house and Uranus in his twelfth (health) house, though they do not form a T-cross. The Sun also opposes Pluto in his fourth house (conditions surrounding death) where this opposition does form a T-cross, though a weak one with Uranus at its focal point. Finally, let us note also that the annular total eclipse of April 18, 1977, the one affecting his chart at his time of death at 28° Aries was in partile conjunction with Uranus. Now, let's look at the facts.

Elvis Presley was born to Vernon and Gladys Presley, the second-born of twins. His brother, Jessie, was stillborn due in part to the very poor living conditions of his family and lack of proper medical attention at the time of this birth. While Elvis was still young the family moved to Memphis, which Elvis claimed as his home for the rest of his life.

At the age of nineteen, Elvis made his first record (reportedly using a guitar that cost $12.50) and was soon signed to a $35,000-per-year recording contract. Shortly thereafter, in 1956, he came to national attention when he appeared twice on the Ed Sullivan Show on television. From there his career rocketed him to the position of the "King of Rock-and-Roll" around the world. He set the style for all of the rock superstars that would follow him.

In 1958 he entered the Army where he refused a plush opportunity to join Special Services and instead specialized in tank repair. He married his wife, Pricilla Ann, in 1967, but was divorced from her in 1972, though it is reported he always remained in love with her. There was one child, a girl, from this marriage. During his life he was always very close to his mother until her death at age forty-two.

Elvis Presley also died at age forty-two, as he had foretold

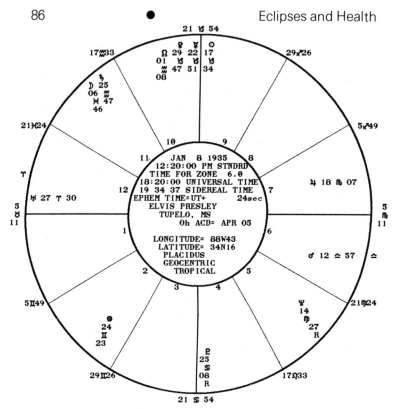

Chart 4: Elvis Presley

on several occasions to close associates, on August 16, 1977, in Memphis, Tennesee. His body was discovered in his bedroom at 2:30 PM by his road manager, Joe Esposito, who vainly tried to restore Elvis's breathing. He was pronounced dead shortly thereafter on arrival at the hospital.

During the last few years of his life, Elvis had put on considerable weight, which it is reported caused hypertension and coronary artery disease. In the coroner's report, his death was attributed to cardiac arythmia (irregular heartbeat). Though he had been known to rely heavily on drugs, drugs were said not to be involved as a cause of death. According to the coroner, who attempted to fix the time of death, Elvis could have died five to six hours earlier than 2:30 PM, but the coroner was unable to fix an exact time, which is unfortunate for our purposes. It is also interesting, from a medical point of view, to note that Elvis had an irrational fear of flying in airplanes which kept him from touring overseas, and in his later years a paranoid fear of others trying to kill him.

Now that we have at least a cursory medical history on Elvis Presley, let's see what information we can get from his horoscope. First and foremost, for purposes of this book, the current eclipse was a partile conjunction with his natal Uranus in Aries in his twelfth (health) house. In Saros series 15, it was ruled by 24° of Gemini. Uranus is at the apex of his cardinal T-cross involving the Sun (vitality and life force) in the ninth house and Pluto retrograde in Cancer in the fourth house (conditions surrounding death). The accompanying partial lunar eclipse on April 4 occurred at 14° Libra, conjunct Mars (square his Sun) in his sixth house. Note also the Moon-Neptune opposition in the fifth/eleventh house polarity, ruled by Leo/Aquarius, for this also figures prominently in the medical picture.

To understand cardiac arythmia the most authoritative source we can turn to is *The Encyclopedia of Medical Astrology* by Dr. H.L. Cornell, M.D. Under "Rhythm —Heart" we discover that cardiac arythmia is symbolized by afflictions along the Leo/Aquarius axis (Moon opposite Neptune in houses five/eleven ruled by Leo/Aquarius), Uranus square Mercury, Saturn in the fixed sign of Aquarius, Venus square Uranus. In medical astrology the Aries/Libra axis controls the body's regulative functions, one of which is heartbeat, controlled by the medulla in the Aries region of the body. Mars is in the sixth house in Libra, its detriment, and Mars symbolizes rhythm. It also squares Mercury, the ruler of the sixth house.

Planets in detriment often relate to fears and phobias. Mars is in the air sign of Libra—thus, the potential for fear of flying in the air. Mars has no beneficial aspects except a biquintile to the Moon.

Note that the potential for Elvis's problem exists in his natal chart. It will take both transits and eclipse positions to activate this potential. The eclipse position cocks the gun, so to speak, and the transit of the Moon pulls the trigger.

In Elvis's case, the conjunction of the solar eclipse at 28° Aries with Uranus and its accompanying lunar eclipse at 14° Libra conjunct Mars cocked the gun. Now let's see what pulled the trigger.

On August 16, 1977, we discover that the transiting Sun opposes natal Saturn (in Leo/Aquarius again!). Transiting Pluto is in partile conjunction with natal Mars (12° Libra 13' versus

12° Libra 57 '). Mercury, afflictor of Mars, is conjunct Neptune at 18° Virgo. Saturn opposes its natal position. Transiting Sun and Saturn are conjunct in Leo (the heart) opposing natal Saturn.

Now, all it takes is the Moon, the timer of events as they occur in our lives, to actually pull the trigger. It's too bad we don't know Elvis's exact time of death to verify the following. However, on the day and at the approximate time of Elvis's death, the Moon was conjunct Neptune at 14° Virgo, and Neptune rules Elvis's twelfth house. On August 16, the Moon was moving at 13° 13 ' per day, 793 ' per day, or 33.04 ' per hour. At 7:00 AM CDT in Memphis, Tennessee, the Moon was at 12° Virgo 52 '. The Moon reached exact conjunction with Elvis's natal Neptune at 10:30 AM CDT. I would therefore suggest that Elvis died at that time, which is well within the limits established by the coroner.

I am quite sure that many astrologers have, by this time, examined the astrological conditions surrounding the death of Elvis Presley. But if they have not considered the position of the current solar and lunar eclipse, how much information can their analysis yield? Does not this added information concerning the eclipse positions clarify the picture? I think the answer is obvious.

I am sure that there are many astrologers who will object by saying that one isolated case like this does not establish an astrological law. I agree. This is only one case. However, the more curious among my readers will, I hope, now be tempted to look at a lot of other cases of death by various means and add eclipse positions to their analyses.

I certainly would never have predicted Elvis Presley's death, had I known of these astrological events. I do not believe that any astrologer should predict death. On the other hand, I do not agree with Evangeline Adams that God did not mean for us to know the day and time of our death. God gave us a mind to use and the symbolism of the stars and planets to study. I cannot believe that God has hidden from us any information that a truly inquiring mind can discern from the facts. While we should not predict death based on the minimal information we now have of an astrological nature regarding death, this does not mean we should not approach the subject with an inquiring mind. God has not drawn any lines, so far as I can tell, around matters surrounding death. And I, for one, will continue to investigate this matter as far as I can. I hope that you will too.

However, let us suppose for the moment that Elvis Presley had come to you as a client and asked you for a forecast for 1977. What advice would you have given him?

If he had consulted me, I would have advised him to pay careful attention to health matters for the next year, to minimize the use of drugs (Neptune), to make sure that his diet included sufficient amounts of iron (Mars) and potassium (for his heart). I would have inquired about potential hypertension (Uranus in Aries in the twelfth), advised a minimum of sugar in the diet (Venus as hidden ruler of Mars) and a glucose tolerance test for potential hypoglycemia. I would have suggested minimizing stressful situations until the eclipse pattern passed from the sixth/twelfth house axis, since his chart suggests that he was under great stress. I would also have suggested that he have all of his bodily regulative functions checked carefully by a competent medical authority of his choice. However, under no circumstances would I have suggested to him that he was going to die! Had he allowed others to care for him, under this twelfth house eclipse emphasis, he might have lived. However, not being a medical doctor, I would have refrained from giving Elvis medical advice. This is not our province as astrologers at this stage of our knowlege.

On the other hand, had his doctor consulted me, I would certainly have suggested that he advise Elvis to submit to more constant attention by those who care for him, a glucose tolerance test, careful diet control (Virgo on the sixth house) and watch out for unexpected accidents during Pluto's transit of Mars.

I do not think that you or any other person can predict his own death. But this does not mean that we are barred from studying the conditions surrounding death or any other matter that surrounds our existence on this Earth.

A series of eclipses across your sixth/twelfth house axis does not necessarily signify death. Most people survive this emphasis. All I would suggest to you is that you pay particular attention to health matters when this eclipse pattern affects your own natal horoscope. There is no substitute for good nutrition and preventive medicine under such emphasis.

11   ●   Case Studies

Corporate Crisis

The only real proof for any astrological theory is, Does it work in real life? Or, to put it another way, can I test the theory out in my own life and convince myself that it really works? Up to this point we've been talking theory. Now let's test the theory out in practice. To do so here we will use the case study method of which the social psychologists are so fond. The material in this chapter was originally published as an article in *Astrology Now*, commissioned by Noel Tyl who, throughout my research on eclipses, has been a continual source of encouragement for me and "a lamp unto my feet."

Several years ago, I was presented with an unusual opportunity to test out my ideas about eclipses. It was a very personal experience for me and yet also one shared by many. I want to share it with you now, not only to demonstrate the eclipse effect, but to encourage other astrologers who have similar experiences to share them with students of astrology everywhere.

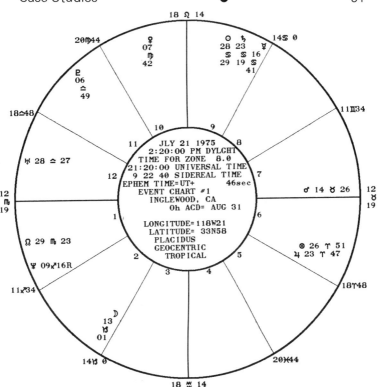

18 ♌ 14

20♍44

♀
07
♍
42

♇
06
♎
49

18♎48

☉ ♄
28 23
♋ ♋ 16
29 19 ♋
41

14♋ 0

11♊34

⛢ 28 ♎ 27

10   9

11 JLY 21 1975
2:20:00 PM DYLGHT
TIME FOR ZONE 8.0
21:20:00 UNIVERSAL TIME
12   9 22 40 SIDEREAL TIME
EPHEM TIME=UT+ 46sec
EVENT CHART #1
INGLEWOOD, CA
0h ACD= AUG 31
1
LONGITUDE=118W21
LATITUDE= 33N58
PLACIDUS
GEOCENTRIC
2   TROPICAL

8

7

6

♂ 14 ♉ 26

12
♉
19

⊗ 26 ♈ 51
♃ 23 ♈ 47

12
♏
19

♌ 29 ♏ 23

♆ 09♐16R

11♐34

3   4   5

18♈48

☽
13
♑
01

20♓44

14♑ 0

18 ♒ 14

Chart 5: Layoff Announcement

On July 21, 1975, a major multinational corporation, whose name has become a byword for all of us, a corporation involved in the manufacture of sophisticated electronic equipment, for whom I was employed, made a momentous corporate decision. The members of the board of directors decided to abandon a large portion of that business as unprofitable. The effect of this decision was that approximately 3,400 people were laid off. Many of these people were employed in Inglewood, California and I was one of them! These employees were notified of this decision at approximately 2:20 PM PDT on July 21, 1975. Chart 5 is the horoscope of this announcement.

I was employed in a middle management position, and as it happened, I had in my files the horoscopes of a number of other middle managers who had previously asked me to cast their horoscopes. To all of us this announcement was totally unpredictable. It was a surprise, to say the least, although we

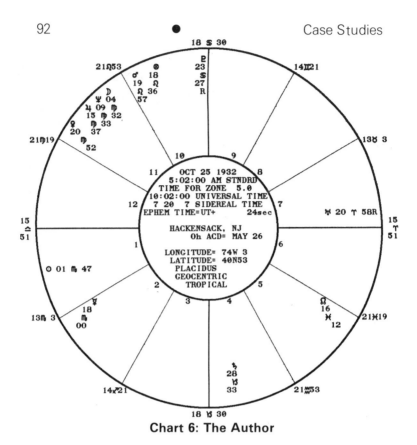

Chart 6: The Author

should have been forwarned by such articles as those in the *Wall Street Journal* that referred to our division as a "corporate play-toy." As none of us had any control over it, the decision was fatalistic. It was also intense in its effect upon the lives of those who were affected by it. Every one of the employees affected was suddenly faced with a crisis in his life.

You might well ask, Who has time to fool around with astrology in the face of such a crisis? Let me assure you that for most of the people involved, this was indeed a crisis. I heard such questions asked as, "How shall I pay for my medical bills? my house? my car? my boat? my children's college education?" Nevertheless it did occur to me that I was being presented with a near-ideal situation in which to study the effect of a single event on the lives of individuals whose horoscopes I knew accurately. Since the actual layoff did not take effect until September 5, 1975, I had adequate opportunity to discuss with many of the people involved just how they personally reacted to this sudden layoff.

Chart 6 is my own horoscope. If you compare chart 5 with chart 6 you will see that transiting Saturn in chart 5 is partile Pluto in chart 6: 23° Capricorn 19′ compared to 23° Capricorn 27′ retrograde. At the same time you will also note that the current eclipse emphasis in my chart (at 20° Taurus) was clearly an eighth house phenomenon by whatever house system you choose to use. It forewarns of an income crisis in mid-1975.

These two factors alone, transiting Saturn conjunct natal Pluto and an eighth house eclipse, indicate a change in professional status and a crisis related to income. Now, add to this the fact that Pluto rules the second house (chart 6), and it's obvious.

Fortunately, this astrological combination did not come as a complete surprise to me. I expcted some sort of financial/professional crisis on or about this date. Thus I had prepared for it by minimizing expenditures and reducing debt months before this inevitable astrological occurrence. Others, not astrologically inclined, did not fare so well, I am sorry to report.

Chart 7 is the horoscope of my immediate superior. He never felt this crisis in financial terms. In his chart the eclipse effect at 20° Taurus was in his eleventh house. At no time did I ever hear him express any personal concern; his constant concern was for the welfare of others. He assisted in every way possible those for whom he was personally responsible and others to whom he could be of special service. Had this been a battlefield instead of a layoff I would gladly have nominated this man for a Distinguished Service Cross. Fortunately, he quickly found another job in which his abilities were appreciated and rewarded. Eleventh house eclipse emphasis are the stuff from which heroes are made! Compare chart 5 with chart 7. Mercury is in partile conjunction to Jupiter (0°6′ from exact). How would you assess this combination? In addition, the Moon in chart 5 is in partile opposition (0°26′ from exact) to Mars, ruler of the eleventh house, which is under the eclipse emphasis in chart 7. This man saw the layoff as a personal challenge, with the heavy transit emphasis upon his first house planets, transiting Moon opposing Mars and squaring Uranus temporarily setting up a cardinal T-Cross with Uranus at its focal point in the eleventh house. The personal challenge was thus focused on Uranus and it became, How can I help others?

●

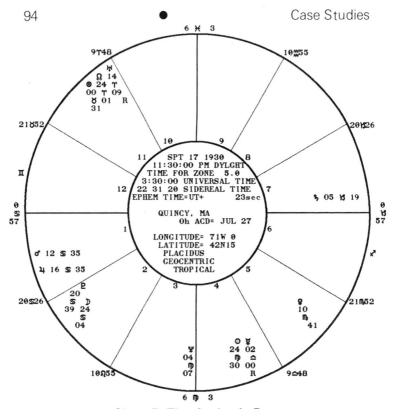

Chart 7: The Author's Boss

Many astrologers feel that the eleventh house symbolizes unexpected events, so it should not escape our attention that in chart 7 there was a decided eleventh house emphasis at this time.

In chart 7 there is also a financial emphasis set up by transit. Pluto and the Moon in chart 7 become the focal point of a second T-cross completed by the transiting opposition in chart 5 of Jupiter opposed to Uranus. He was thus also concerned with the question, How can I conserve my tangible resources?

Chart 8 is that of another manager who, at the age of forty-three, had invested nearly twelve years of his professional career with the company. He was a talented specialist in the design and marketing of electronic equipment and a man whom others considered on his way to becoming a divisional vice-president within four or five years. In his horoscope the eclipse emphasis falls within his twelfth house. This house is natally emphasized containing Uranus as the focal point of his

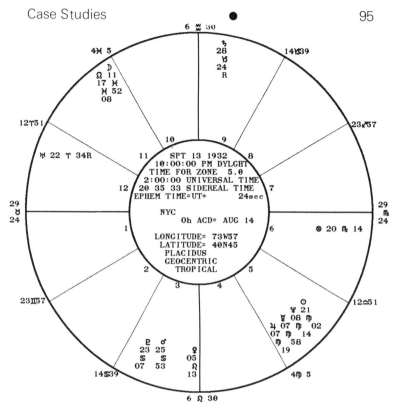

6 ♒ 30

4♓ 5
☽
☊ 11
17 ♓
♓ 52
08

28
♄
24
R

14♑39

12♈51

23♐57

♆ 22 ♈ 34R

10

9

SPT 13 1932
10:00:00 PM DYLGHT
TIME FOR ZONE 5.0
2:00:00 UNIVERSAL TIME
20 35 33 SIDEREAL TIME
EPHEM TIME=UT+ 24sec

NYC
0h ACD= AUG 14

LONGITUDE= 73W57
LATITUDE= 40N45
PLACIDUS
GEOCENTRIC
TROPICAL

11

12

1

2

8

7

6

5

⊗ 20 ♏ 14

29
♉
24

29
♏
24

23♊57

3

4

12♎51

♇ ♂
23 25
♋ ♋
07 53

♀
05
♌
13

14♋39

☉
♆ 21
☿ 08 ♍
♃ 07 ♍ 02
07 ♍ 14
♍ 58
19

4♍ 5

6 ♌ 30

Chart 8: Another Manager

cardinal T-cross, which accounts for his interest in electrȯnïċ (Uranus) research (twelfth house).

If the sixth house symbolizes the favors we do for others, the twelfth house represents the favors others do for us. He viewed this announcement quite fatalistically (twelfth house) and ultimately as a favor from the company, since it pushed him in the direction he felt he was headed anyway, the organization of his own business. The new business was, of course, to be a partnership (lunar eclipse point in his seventh house).

Between the event chart, (chart 5) and his horoscope (chart 8) there are *seven* transiting contacts with natal points with orbs of less than one degree! Transiting Venus is conjunct Mercury (orb = 16′), Neptune (orb = 23′) and Jupiter (orb = 23′) and opposed to the Moon (orb = 10′). Transiting Jupiter is conjunct natal Uranus (orb = 1°13′). Transiting Saturn is conjunct natal Pluto (orb = 12′), and transiting Sun is opposed to natal Saturn (orb = 5 '). July 21 was an auspicious date for this man.

Let us pause here for a moment and note several significant points about all of these example charts. All show a Saturn-Pluto contact. Pluto is importantly involved in all of these charts, and for good reason. Our business involved electronic replication (or duplication) and Pluto is the planet symbolic of this process. The unexpected fatalistic character of this announcement is related in some way to the twelfth house in each chart, usually to a transit or eclipse point contact with the ruler of, or a planet in, the twelfth house. These two points hold true for the nearly two dozen horoscopes in my complete study.

The solar eclipse of which we have been speaking was a partial one that occurred on May 11, 1975, in Saros series 13 at the Moon's south node, under the control of 6° Gemini. It was accompanied by a total lunar eclipse at 4° Sagittarius that occurred on May 25. The solar eclipse occurred at 20° Taurus.

In the event chart, (chart 5) we find the solar eclipse in the seventh house and we also find many of the employees who were laid off forming small businesses in partnerships with others. The lunar eclipse fell in the first house of the event chart and we find many of these people suddenly facing identity crises. The event chart must be considered as overlayed upon all of the individual charts we study that were affected by this announcement.

With 6° Gemini as the point that influences all Saros series 13 south nodal eclipses, it is interesting to see where this point falls in the example charts and the influence it has, albeit of a secondary nature. In my own chart, chart 6, it fell in the eighth house, along with the solar eclipse point. In chart 7 it fell in the twelfth house, again showing the influence of twelfth house matters on this chart. In chart 8 it fell in the first house suggesting a secondary crisis of identity.

I find it especially helpful in working with eclipses to refer to one or more books that give the specific symbolism of each degree of the zodiac, Dhi Manthri's *The Degrees of Life* for example. In this book, for 6° of Gemini we find, "Thy personal labors and thy manners open to thee many doors bearing great seals in many unfrequented corridors. Thy pen and thy voice assist thy purposes; thy discrimination leadeth thee far." In terms of my own personal horoscope, these words have had great meaning for me since the time of this event.

For 20° Taurus we read, "Wealth of others is often in thy keeping; protect it well. Rest is neither thy desire nor thy lot for thou canst accomplish but a part of that thou seest to be done." To this I can only shout a loud "Amen!" Almost every one of my subjects in this study went on to jobs that involved the handling of the money and/or the possessions of others, e.g., a travel agency, a business consulting firm, a cost accountant and a cost effectiveness manager. As a writer and publisher this also speaks to my own horoscope, especially about accomplishing only a part of what I see needs to be done!

For 4° Sagittarius we read, "In thy latter portion of life [presumably beyond forty], position and responsibility are thine, and thou canst then employ thy powerful imagination, thine inventive capacity, and thy swiftly changing thought in furtherance of thy ventures." Again, generally through partnerships, most of the people in my study have accepted positions of greater responsibility, requiring imagination and inventive genius of one sort or another in order to survive and advance themselves.

While this chapter is not meant to be a full-blown scientific study but rather a guide to using the eclipse points in your own predictions, it is interesting to consider the charts of two employees who were not laid off on September 5, but were temporarily retained to wind down the affairs of the division. They knew that an eventual layoff in 1976 was inevitable, but for the time being the corporation needed them. Consider these persons controls, if you will, in our experiment. Both charts lack the Saturn-Pluto contact for the time being, but both experience this contact when Saturn reaches 8° of Leo in mid-1976, the time that they expect to be laid off. On or about August 13, 1976 when Saturn reached 8° Leo they were in fact released too. Chart 9 is that of my closest co-worker. The solar eclipse falls in his eighth house, the companion lunar eclipse, in his second house. His major concern at the time of the announcement was financial. He had just purchased an expensive home whose upkeep cost over twenty-five per cent of his income. For him the question was, "How can I continue to pay my bills?"

A transit of Pluto over the natal ascendant is one of the heaviest and most important transits that can occur in anyone's lifetime. If you have Libra or Virgo rising you

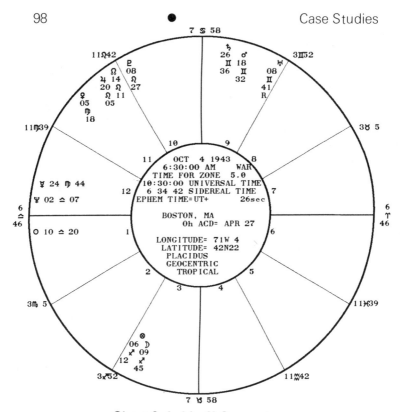

Chart 9: Laid-off Co-worker

already know or will shortly discover what I am talking about.
In chart 9 we find Pluto within one minute of the ascendant at
6° Libra 48'. Transiting Neptune is also within 36' of exact
opposition to natal Uranus. However, there are no other important transiting contacts for July 21. The twelfth house is
again directly involved, natal Neptune is in the twelfth house
along with Mercury, ruler of the ninth and twelfth houses.
Layoff seems inevitable when transiting Saturn reaches natal
Pluto at 8° Leo 27'.

Finally, chart 10 is that of another person who was temporarily retained but whose ultimate layoff was also in the
cards under the transit of Saturn to natal Pluto. In this case,
the solar eclipse falls in his first house and its companion lunar
eclipse in his seventh. I cannot ethically discuss the details of
this situation except to say that he went through an identity
crisis at this time and a real test of his somewhat shaky marriage. In his horoscope there are no auspicious transiting con-

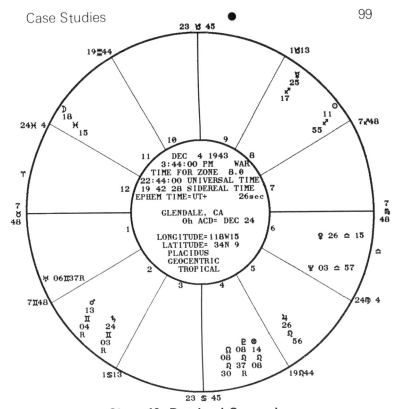

Chart 10: Retained Co-worker

tacts with chart 5 at all. However, on April 29, 1976, a solar eclipse of the Sun at 9° Taurus 20 ′ occurred in conjunction with his natal ascendant. He and his wife shortly thereafter went through marriage counseling, and today the marriage seems stronger than ever. He finally discovered himself and what he had been doing to others under this solar eclipse emphasis and he corrected many of his faults.

It is important to notice that in all of these charts a crisis with its inevitable review process took place whether or not the solar eclipse point fell in conjunction or in opposition to a natal planetary position. Most of the previous writers on this subject have said that eclipses cause problems only when they make intimate contact with a natal point in the horoscope. My own observation does not confirm this at all. However, when there is a contact (orb = ± 5°) the crisis generated takes on more emphasis and importance.

The Use of Eclipses with Relocation Charts

A relocation chart is a horoscope drawn for the date and time of birth but using the geographical location where the subject currently lives rather than the place of birth. Unless there has been a move of considerable distance from the birthplace, there is not much difference between the relocation chart and the natal horoscope. If you've never done a relocation chart for yourself, however, it is worth doing and certainly worth comparing to your natal chart in terms of eclipse effects.

I use eclipse locations with relocation charts. Chart 11 is my own relocation chart from my birthplace in New Jersey to Van Nuys, California, a move of about 2,600 miles from my place of birth that makes a considerable change in the houses when compared with my basic natal horoscope (chart 2) as you can quickly see.

The solar eclipse at 20° Taurus falls in the ninth house of the relocation chart. The lunar eclipse falls in the third house. This illustrates the principal clearly.

The crisis had its main impact upon the eighth house of the natal chart (chart 6). Had I been living close to my birth location the crisis would have been financial and that would have been that. However, I was living far enough away from my birthplace for the relocation chart to have an overlay effect upon the natal chart.

I did not begin writing until I moved to California, a move which shifted Mercury from the second to the third house. With this move Mercury rather than Venus became the chart ruler. Neptune and all that it implies has certainly worked its subtle effects, coming into almost exact conjunction with the ascendant in the relocation chart. With Mars in the twelfth house of the relocation chart I have had the opportunity to devote considerably more time and energy to research; and with the Sun now in the second house I have been able to develop new talents.

Add to this the solar eclipse of May 11, 1975, just before the layoff, which falls in the ninth house (publishing, among other things), and it becomes obvious in which direction I would choose to go. Writing and publishing have become my full-time occupation since this time.

How important is the relocation chart? In my experience, it

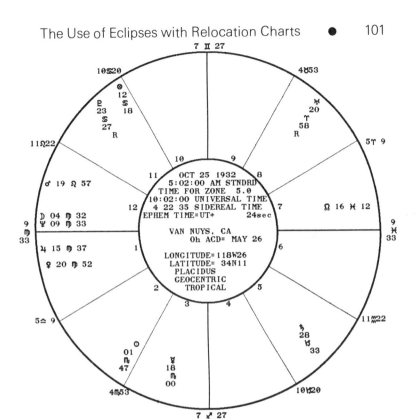

Chart 11: Relocation Chart for the Author

can and usually does give a significant indication of how the natal chart should be delineated, not only in terms of eclipses but also in terms of transits. The relocation chart becomes an overlay on the natal chart in delineation and in my opinion should not be ignored.

My own experience is not an isolated case. I have seen similar effects occur in every other relocation chart that I have studied, the effect becoming more striking and significant the farther away from home the individual has chosen to relocate. Does it then surprise you that so many people born on the east coast report that they have found a whole new way of life for themselves in California?

12 ● Eclipses in Transit

In this chapter we will concern ourselves with the interpretations that should be given when a solar eclipse is found to be in either conjunction or opposition to a planet or point in the natal horoscope.

First, some general remarks and observations.

Orb of Aspect The question, What orb do you use for aspects? is one of the most frequently asked by students of their instructors. The rule that I shall give you here is an arbitrary one, based upon my own personal observations of eclipse effects. I find that by using an orb of ± 5°, I get the information that I am seeking. I do not recommend using a wider orb, but perhaps you'd prefer to tighten up a bit on the orb I recommend and limit it to, say, ± 3°. Whatever orb you choose to use, the closer the aspect, the stronger the effect. An opposition or conjunction of an eclipse point and a natal point within an orb of ± 1° is going to be much stronger in effect than if the orb were ± 2° or ± 3°. I hope you will eventually arrive at your own conclusion and not arbitrarily accept my limits of ± 5° as being necessarily correct.

What House is the Eclipse Point in? In your synthesis of the following descriptions for the planets, ask yourself first, What house is the eclipse in? In what house polarity? What types of crises does this house polarity symbolize? Is this point above or below the horizon line, and what does this signify in terms of need? You may wish to review chapter 6 to fix these crises possibilities in your mind.

What Sign is the Eclipse Point In? The sign location and its quadruplicity and elemental significance cannot be under-rated. The tendency if in a cardinal sign will be to meet the crisis head-on and accept it as a personal challenge; if in a fixed sign, to try and live with the crisis and maintain the status quo; if in a mutable sign, to either work around the crisis or pretend that the crisis does not exist. The sign element will indicate on what level the crisis and emphasis of the eclipse will be most strongly felt: a fire sign indicates a crisis of the spirit and a challenge felt very personally; an earth sign in-dicates a crisis on the physical level in terms of tangible and real things; an air sign indicates an intellectual crisis, a challenge to the thought processes; and a water sign indicates an emotional crisis or one that involves intangible matters.

What Sign and Degree Rules the Saros Series? I hope that you will get into the habit of referring to chapter 4 in your analyses of eclipses to determine the basic nature of the Saros series for each eclipse. Get yourself a good reference book on the symbolism of each of the degrees of the zodiac and use it for a background analysis of what each eclipse portends. The ancient astrologers did this long before Ptolemy, and I think that it's time we at least tested their rules for applicability on the modern scene.

Keeping these points in mind as a minimum prior to your in-depth analysis of the effect of an eclipse point, we are now ready to proceed to the question of what conjunctions and op-positions to the positions of natal planets portend in our lives.

Sun

Conjunction This invariably signals a crisis of major im-portance in our lives. Most people remark under this conjunction, "Thank God this eclipse occurs only once every eighteen years or so!" The challenge goes right to the heart of things, to the ego. It signals the need to review all those things you hold most precious and dear and to sort out the junk. You will feel that you are being pulled in a dozen different directions at the same time. The real need is to begin to assign priorities to those things that are more important to you in life and give the most important things priority attention. You've reached a fork in the road of life, and now you must choose which fork to follow, like it or not, and be willing to accept the consequences of your choice. There will be no going back to retrace your steps if you make what seems to be the wrong choice. If you accept this choice willingly, anticipating it ahead of time and controlling matters very carefully in terms of its house location, then you have a wonderful opportunity to bring added zest into your life. If you fight the crisis, events will likely leave you kicking and screaming about what life has done to you.

Opposition   During its period of effect, this eclipse presents you with a real challenge to the ego. You face the fact that you are not always right and that there exists an alternative way of accomplishing your purposes. You have a real opportunity under this eclipse to approach your problems from a fresh perspective. You don't have to choose this alternative approach to things if you don't want to, but you will have to accept the results of your choice, whatever it might be. It is like a breath of fresh air blown into a stuffy room. You can shut it out or let it in. But whatever you decide to do, it's your choice and you must live with the consequences. It can be a golden opportunity to get out of a rut, or you can choose to defend your rut against all challengers. It is up to you.

Moon

Conjunction   Be it a conjunction or opposition, under this eclipse emphasis you are faced with your past. This is a period of great personal testing of the foundations upon which you've built your life. If the foundation is secure and built on solid rock, you've no need to fear. If it is built on sand, then likely you're in trouble. You have the opportunity to move your house to a new foundation based upon more solid stuff, or you can just stand by and watch it crumble into rubble.

Your public image is going to come in for some careful scrutiny here. If society considers you to be a valuable person, they'll let you know it under this eclipse. If they don't think much of your efforts, society will let you know that, too. Your habit patterns are going to come in for some close scrutiny too. If the habits are beneficial to you, they will be reinforced; if they are harmful or bad habit patterns, you'll have the opportunity to change them. In any case, you're going to have to defend those things that you hold most dear. However, when this trial period is over, you're likely to be a better person from having undergone this experience.

Opposition In the manner of the house polarity involved, you are going to have your personal relationships with others tested under this influence. The emotions can get heavily involved in this testing period. Not infrequently the mother is involved, either directly or indirectly, and there is a testing by you of the precepts, principles and general programing impressed upon you by your mother in your early years. If this programing still works and has relevance in your life, it will be strengthened; if there are flaws in the program, you have the opportunity to change and correct them. Under this transit, mama's boys suddenly find their manhood, younger folks often rebel against parental authority, the perfect child suddenly becomes unmanageable. Problems and needs related to the location of the solar eclipse are frequently perceived in terms of the opposite house. For example, a second house eclipse symbolizes the need to share tangible things like money, but you perceive the crisis as a need to add to your possessions, or you blame an identity crisis (first house) on your partner (seventh house). This opposition sensitizes you to the quid pro quo in the related house polarity, "If I do this what will you do for me in return?"

Mercury

Conjunction This crisis relates to more than the thinking process, the intellect and communications—those things we normally associate with the symbolism of Mercury. It goes deeper. There is undoubtedly an intellectual crisis, and ideas that you previously held sacred may be revealed as sheer stupidity. For a time under this influence you will cast about looking for new sacred cows to replace those that you've lost.

The deeper challenge is to begin thinking now for the first time about things that you've never really thought about or scrutinized before. It can also be a time for you to discover that you can have intellectual pleasures as well as physical pleasures. You can sharpen your perception of the things around you, little things you've never noticed before. Look for the humor as well as the pathos in life. Increase your light conversational abilities. Begin writing that book you've always planned to write someday. Give the child in you a chance to come out and play. Many adults, as they grow older, forget how to play. Everthing they do must have deep meaning and purpose. Now is the time to rediscover how to play again. Most especially, talk about, think about and play around with those things related to the natal position by house of Mercury in your chart.

Opposition　The opposition of the solar eclipse to Mercury is quite different from the conjunction. You won't have much time for play now. You will find yourself running about trying to straighten out things that have gotten off the track because someone else has misunderstood what you have said. Communications get garbled. You'll say one thing and others will often get quite a different message. Children can often become a source of irritation. Others will want to play when you want to get down to some serious work. Many people feel that they are under increased stress and strain during this period. Your thinking and ideas related to the house position of natal Mercury will be directly challenged by others. It seems that every time you want to do something someone else will put a barrier in your path. Disagreements will arise relating to deeds, leases and contracts—often they will require re-negotiation or alteration. However, things are not as bleak as they may appear. You are again being tested, as happens under all oppositions, by others in matters related to this house polarity. They will force you to rethink your position on a lot of things, which is really quite healthy for you in the long run. You can really begin to appreciate and re-examine things that you've been taking for granted, and then make alterations that you think proper or are more comfortable with. When you attempt to communicate with others, have them repeat back to you what you've just said to be sure that they've gotten the correct message. This is a good habit anyway, and now is a fine time to develop it.

Venus

Conjunction While Venus as a planetary energy is often thought of as being passive, eclipses to its position are not. They can take on the nature of a first-rate crisis and become very painful if you fail to pay attention to what this crisis is telling you, especially in terms of the house in which it occurs. Here's why. In whatever house natal Venus is found in your horoscope, you have a kind of guardian angel watching over you. It's not that you can do no wrong in matters of this house, rather, it's that when you do err you've got the guardian angel there to throw you a rope. Under this eclipse conjunction suddenly the guardian angel has disappeared and you have to make it on your own for a change with no help. The conjunction with Venus is more related to how well you like yourself, your own self-image, and this comes in for considerable scrutiny under this influence. This ought also to be a time not only for re-evaluating those things that bring you the greatest pleasure in life but also for doing them. Indulge yourself a bit. Do what brings you pleasure. You've earned it. If you've not already done so, stop and evaluate those things that give you the greatest pleasure and satisfaction in life. Far too many people feel somehow guilty about indulging themselves in activities that give them happiness and satisfaction. If this is you, it's now time to deal with that guilt and put it out of your life, now and forever after. Start loving yourself more than you do now, and stop feeling guilty about it.

Opposition Under this transit, you are not dealing with self-love but rather with your love for others and their love for you. Under this influence you can suddenly imagine that no one loves you anymore. Or, that every time you want to do something that gives you pleasure, other people or events keep getting in your way. Things that you treasure can sometimes get lost for a time. You want to take some time to stop and smell the flowers in whatever space is yours and someone keeps "raining on your parade." What to do? Get out your umbrella and wait for the shower to pass. A bit more tolerance of others is now called for. Start looking for those things that will bring pleasure to others for a change and the payoff for you can be greater than you might imagine. Indulge yourself under the conjunction; indulge others under the opposition.

Certain compromises, as always under oppositions, will be called for. Don't sell yourself short or become a doormat for someone else. Love affairs do get terminated, certainly tested, under such oppositions, but when this crisis has passed, no matter how it eventually turns out, you can be sure that you will be the better for having gone through it. That's why this eclipse review process is so important in our lives. It provides us with an opportunity for new growth and development.

Mars

Conjunctions Mars deals with how you use and express your physical energies, and under this conjunction you're going to have to pay closer attention to this process. If you're the type of person who is constantly on the run, you are going to have to give yourself a chance to slow down a bit or you are asking for physical problems. If you've not taken sufficient physical exercise, you are going to have to start doing so now, or you are asking for trouble. If you've forgotten that you are also a physical being, with certain physical needs and desires, you're going to be reminded of it under this conjunction. Neglect these warnings and you become accident-prone, angry, especially at yourself, argumentative with others and perhaps even violent. The quiet little mouse can sometimes start to roar. Whether you come out of this crisis scared or with your batteries well recharged is up to you. It's a case of how you use your physical energies during this period, constructively or destructively. One thing is certain: if you don't look carefully at and deal with any anger you've been covering up or denying, it's going to come out somewhere in a very destructive manner. Either you handle this energy consciously, or it will handle you subconsciously. Now is the time to really apply that Mars energy to matters related to the house polarity of natal Mars. Try to do it daily during this period and you may well find that you've established a fine new habit and method of dealing with your frustrations.

Oppositions As you might well expect, this can be a period of warfare with others. Compromise? Never! That's how you're likely to feel, and as long as you are unwilling to unbend no one else is likely to either. This opposition can put lots of zest and zing into your life. If you like the challenge of combat, pitting yourself against others to test yourself and your mettle, you can bet that this is going to be an exciting time for you. There's nothing wrong with this as long as your warfare is of a constructive nature, as in athletic competition. Let it become destructive, however, or turn this destructive energy in upon yourself, and you'll get yourself in lots of trouble. I've seen cases where people have turned this period into the most productive period in thier lives, when they've suddenly decided to face up to the competition and "Damn the torpedoes, full speed ahead!" I also have some examples in my files of people who've attempted and sometimes succeeded in committing suicide under this influence. The point is, the energy is there demanding that it be used and you've got to find the proper target for it. Not infrequently this becomes a period of increased sexual activity. Those who have been denying proper sexual expression in their lives suddenly feel that it can be denied no longer, that it's got to come out somewhere. And that somewhere is where you've got to pay careful attention or it will surely get you into trouble. Again, finding the proper target for its expression is the problem.

Jupiter

Conjunction   Jupiter's basic symbolism is that of growth and expansion as well as good luck. Overoptimism during this period is your greatest enemy. The temptation is to overextend yourself and occupy new space that you cannot hold or protect. With the conjunction you may be your own greatest enemy, though you will be tempted to blame your failure on others. As I explained at the beginning of this chapter, the level at which this attempted expansion is likely to occur depends upon natal Jupiter's sign position. If, for example, Jupiter is in a fire sign, you may gain spiritual awareness under this emphasis; or, if in an earth sign, you may gain weight. Under the conjunction the motivating force comes from within; it is self-generated. Luck may well come your way in the form of unexpected gain, but you may have difficulty in holding onto this windfall, unless you are careful to protect it. With the good also comes the bad, however, and if Jupiter is a significator in any medical problems you might have, they may take on added significance and importance, too. As problems present themselves, seek out expert advice, do not take the advice given on faith. Test out the advice on the basis of your own prior experience and act accordingly. I have seen many cases under this influence where individuals feel that they have suddenly found their savior, later to become discouraged and disenchanted. You cannot lay your problems on others and through faith come upon a miraculous solution. You've got to deal with them yourself. No guru can do it for you.

Opposition   Under this influence, you are going to feel some real challenges to the space you've occupied in the past. And you'll have competition from others who want to occupy the same space you want. There will also be challenges to your basic faith. If you're a trusting person, you may be disappointed when others are revealed as unworthy of that trust. On the other hand, if you trust no one, you may be forced for the first time in your life to put your trust in someone else. The lesson, of course, is in learning whom you can trust and whom you can't. To put it another way, beware of Trojan horses. Others are going to test your faith, especially in matters that are related to the house containing natal Jupiter. If your faith is strong and well placed, it will survive and be the stronger thereby. If it is misplaced, you'll discover that too and have the opportunity to adjust accordingly. You'll likely get lots of help from others under this opposition. When you do, ask yourself why. The lesson to be learned from Jupiter, or at least one lesson, is the old saying, "You don't get something for nothing."

Saturn

Conjunction   The house polarity of natal Saturn is the area of life where you are going to be faced with your greatest responsibilities in life, and when there is a solar eclipse conjunction natal Saturn, the time has come to accept and shoulder these responsibilities. Saturn deals with form and structure, and sometimes in accepting new responsibilities it becomes necessary to restructure our lives. If you feel frustration, pain and trauma under this contact, you are fighting against your true responsibilities. After all, when we choose to occupy space we are the stewards of that space and responsible for it. When it gets disorganized we know it and feel it. Everything has its price. The more space we choose to occupy, the greater the cost. Under this contact the cosmic bill-collector arrives with the bill for those resources we have consumed in growing. If we have been extravagant, the bill is high, but it is also correct and fair, down to the last penny. Under the conjunction we must accept the responsibility and pay the price for our own actions; under the opposition we must sometimes accept responsibility for the actions of others. If when the eclipse gets to natal Saturn and the bills arrive you already know the cost, its arrival is less upsetting.

Opposition We are sometimes held responsible for the actions of others, expecially those who are under our control, as, for example, minor children or employees. If you are willing to accept the gratuitous benefits of fate (under Jupiter) then you ought to be willing to accept liabilities and responsibilities for the actions of others, as well. The law of compensation works in all things throughout nature. If you've learned to handle Saturn well in its natal house polarity, in your chart, then you may reach a point in life where you will welcome added responsibility when it is thrust upon you, like an unexpected increase in your job responsibilities, often without added compensation at the moment. The eventual payoff is not always in money; sometimes it is in added power. No one ever became more powerful without paying the price: more responsibility. That is why Saturn, Capricorn and the fourth/tenth house polarity all deal in part with the use of power. Saturn often symbolizes the things that we fear, too, and in an opposition from an eclipse to natal Saturn others will sometimes help us to overcome these fears. This contact in the chart should not be anticipated with dread. Rather it should be anticipated as an opportunity to put Saturn's natal house in order with the help of others. A good housecleaning ahead of time will minimize its negative effects when the eclipse eventually arrives, as is inevitable in all of our lives.

Jupiter and Saturn contacts by eclipses remind us of the societal forces at work in our lives. They symbolize opposing but complementary forces in our life: expansion versus restriction, growth versus aging, leisure time versus the responsible use of time, play versus work, the bulls versus the bears. Life becomes less traumatic and more joyful when we learn to balance these powers, one with the other.

Until we have learned to handle the Jupiter-Saturn power duo in our horoscopes and our lives we will hardly be able to understand, let alone benefit from, eclipse contacts with the three outer planets—Uranus, Neptune and Pluto. The prize, however, for doing so is rich beyond measure.

The Outer Planets

Conjunction   In each case of a solar eclipse conjunct an outer planet, if you are attuned to the vibrations of the planet, you have a real opportunity to benefit personally from its energies, but first you have to know how to tune it in, or all you get is static. An eclipse conjunct Uranus offers an opportunity for greater personal freedom and independence; an eclipse conjunct Neptune, an opportunity for greater spiritual understanding and joy; an eclipse conjunct Pluto, an opportunity for transforming the qualities of its house polarity to a higher plane of understanding and being. Misunderstood or misused, Uranus can limit your freedom: Neptune can bring self-deceit, and Pluto can cause decay—all related principally to their house polarity.

Opposition   Basically, the symbolism for the oppositions to these natal points by a solar eclipse is the same as indicated above, with one important exception: under the conjunction what happens is self-induced, while what happens under the opposition is often induced initially by actions taken by others. However, just because action is initiated by someone else does not mean that we are any the less responsible for the ultimate effect upon us.

Retrograde Planets

The question is always raised by the thinking student, How do these eclipse contacts change in their effect upon us when the planet contacted is retrograde? I have not as yet been able to discern the complete answer to this question, but I will share my observations with you, incomplete though they may be. Normally, the energies of retrograde planets have at least a share of their energies expressed or reflected inward upon our nature at the more subconscious levels instead of being focused outward as they are when the planet is direct in motion. I believe that an eclipse in contact with a retrograde planet presents us with an opportunity to get in touch with these subconscious levels and to refocus the energy outward.

Data on Sun, Moon and Earth

Comparative Diameters
Sun	866,400 miles	401.11
Earth	7,926 miles	3.67
Moon	2,160 miles	1

Length of Umbra
Earth	857,000 miles	3.69
Moon	232,000 miles	1

Distance from Earth to Moon
Mean	238,857 miles
Minimum	222,000 miles
Maximum	258,000 miles

Moon's Umbra on Earth's Surface
Maximum diameter: 167 miles
Speed of movement: 1060-5000 miles per hour

Duration of Total Solar Eclipse
Mean	3 minutes
Maximum	7.5 minutes

Diameter of Penumbra
Moon	3,000 miles
Earth	5,700 miles

Moon's Rotation Period about the Earth
Sidereal Period: 27 days, 7 hours, 43 minutes, 11.5 seconds.
Lunar Month: 29 days, 12 hours, 44 minutes, 2.8 seconds.

Movement of Moon's Nodes: 19.5° per year or 3.20 ′ per day (retrograde)

Time of Saros Interval: 6585.3 days or 18 years, 9-11 days (depending upon number of leap years in the interval); 19 returns of sun to same nodal position; 242 returns of Moon to same nodal position; 223 lunar months. Eclipse recurs 120° further west on Earth's surface.

20th Century Solar Eclipses

Columns give date of occurrence, north (N) or south (S) node, longitude, type (T = total, P = partial, A = annular) and saros series.

Year	Date	Node	Longitude	Type	Saros
1900	05/28	S	07°♊	T	10
	11/22	N	00°♐	A	11
1901	05/18	S	27°♉	T	11
	11/11	N	18°♏	A	12
1902	04/08	S	18°♈	P	12
	05/07	S	16°♉	P	12
	10/31	N	07°♏	P	13
1903	03/29	S	07°♈	A	13
	09/21	N	27°♍	T	14
1904	03/17	S	26°♓	A	14
	09/09	N	17°♍	T	15
1905	03/06	S	15°♓	A	15
	08/30	N	06°♍	T	16
1906	02/23	S	04°♓	P	16
	07/21	N	28°♋	P	17
	08/20	N	26°♌	P	17
1907	01/14	S	23°♑	T	17
	07/10	N	17°♋	A	18
1908	01/03	S	12°♑	T	18
	06/28	N	07°♋	A	19
	12/23	S	01°♑	AT	19
1909	06/17	N	26°♊	T	01
	12/12	S	20°♐	P	01
1910	05/09	N	18°♉	T	02
	11/02	S	09°♏	P	02
1911	04/28	N	07°♉	T	03
	10/22	S	28°♎	A	03
1912	04/17	N	27°♈	AT	04
	10/10	S	17°♎	T	04
1913	04/06	N	16°♈	P	05
	03/31	S	08°♍	P	05
	09/30	S	06°♎	P	05
1914	02/25	N	06°♓	A	06
	08/21	S	28°♌	T	06
1915	02/14	N	24°♒	A	07
	08/10	S	17°♌	A	07
1916	02/03	N	14°♒	T	08
	07/30	S	07°♌	A	08
	12/24	N	03°♑	P	09
1917	01/23	N	22°♑	P	09
	06/19	S	28°♊	P	09
	07/19	S	26°♋	P	09
	12/14	N	22°♐	A	10
1918	06/08	S	17°♊	T	10
	12/03	N	11°♐	A	11
1919	05/29	S	07°♊	T	11
	11/22	N	29°♏	A	12
1920	05/18	S	27°♉	P	12
	11/10	N	18°♏	P	13
1921	04/08	S	18°♈	A	13
	10/01	N	08°♎	T	14
1922	03/28	S	07°♈	A	14
	09/21	N	27°♍	T	15
1923	03/17	S	26°♓	A	15
	09/10	N	17°♍	T	16
1924	03/05	S	15°♓	P	16
	07/31	N	08°♌	P	17
	08/30	N	07°♍	P	17
1925	01/24	S	04°♒	T	17
	07/20	N	28°♋	A	18
1926	01/14	S	23°♑	T	18
	07/09	N	17°♋	A	19
1927	01/03	S	12°♑	A	19
	06/29	N	07°♋	T	01
	12/24	S	01°♑	P	01
1928	05/19	N	28°♉	T	02
	06/17	N	26°♊	P	02
	11/12	S	20°♏	P	02

1929	05/09	N	18°♉	T	03		05/30	N	09°♊	P	02
	11/01	S	09°♏	A	03		06/29	N	07°♋	P	02
							11/23	S	01°♐	P	02
1930	04/28	N	08°♉	AT	04						
	10/21	S	28°♎	T	04	1947	05/20	N	28°♉	T	03
							11/12	S	20°♏	A	03
1931	04/18	N	27°♈	P	05						
	09/12	S	18°♍	P	05	1948	05/09	N	18°♉	AT	04
	10/11	S	17°♎	P	05		11/01	S	09°♏	T	04
1932	03/07	N	17°♓	A	06	1949	04/28	N	08°♉	P	05
	08/31	S	08°♍	T	06		10/21	S	28°♎	P	05
1933	02/24	N	06°♓	A	07	1950	03/18	N	28°♓	A	06
	08/21	S	28°♌	A	07		09/12	S	19°♍	T	06
1934	02/14	N	25°♒	T	08	1951	03/07	N	17°♓	A	07
	08/10	S	17°♌	A	08		09/01	S	08°♍	A	07
1935	01/05	N	14°♑	P	09	1952	02/25	N	06°♓	T	08
	02/03	N	14°♒	P	09		08/20	S	28°♌	A	08
	06/30	S	08°♋	P	09	1953	02/14	N	26°♒	P	09
	07/30	S	07°♌	P	09		07/11	S	19°♋	P	09
	12/25	N	03°♑	A	10		08/29	S	17°♌	P	09
1936	06/19	S	28°♊	T	10	1954	01/05	N	14°♑	A	10
	12/13	N	22°♐	A	11		06/30	S	08°♋	T	10
1937	06/08	S	18°♊	T	11		12/25	N	03°♑	A	11
	12/02	N	10°♐	A	12	1955	06/20	S	28°♊	T	11
1938	05/29	S	08°♊	T	12		12/14	N	22°♐	A	12
	11/22	N	29°♏	P	13	1956	06/08	S	18°♊	T	12
1939	04/19	S	29°♈	A	13		12/02	N	10°♐	P	13
	10/12	N	19°♎	T	14	1957	04/29	S	09°♉	T	13
1940	04/07	S	18°♈	A	14		10/23	N	00°♏	P	14
	10/01	N	08°♎	T	15	1958	04/19	S	29°♈	A	14
1941	03/27	S	07°♈	A	15		10/12	N	19°♎	T	15
	09/21	N	28°♍	T	16	1959	04/08	S	18°♈	A	15
1942	03/16	S	26°♓	P	16		10/02	N	09°♎	T	16
	08/12	N	19°♌	P	17	1960	03/27	S	07°♈	P	16
	09/10	N	17°♍	P	17		09/20	N	28°♍	P	17
1943	02/04	S	15°♒	T	17	1961	02/15	S	27°♒	T	17
	08/01	N	08°♌	A	18		08/11	N	19°♌	A	18
1944	01/25	S	05°♒	T	18	1962	02/05	S	16°♒	T	18
	07/20	N	28°♋	A	19		07/31	N	08°♌	A	19
1945	01/14	S	24°♑	A	19	1963	01/25	S	05°♒	A	19
	07/09	N	16°♋	T	01		07/20	N	28°♋	T	01
1946	01/03	S	13°♑	P	01						

```
1964  01/14  S  24°♑  P 01    1982  01/25  S  05°♒  P 01
      06/10  N  20°♊  P 02          06/21  N  00°♋  P 02
      07/09  N  17°♋  P 02          07/20  N  28°♋  P 02
      12/04  S  12°♐  P 02          12/15  S  23°♐  P 02

1965  05/30  N  09°♊  T 03    1983  06/11  N  20°♊  T 03
      11/23  S  01°♐  A 03          12/04  S  12°♐  A 03

1966  05/20  N  28°♉  AT 04  1984  05/30  N  09°♊  AT 04
      11/12  S  20°♏  T 04          11/22  S  01°♐  T 04

1967  05/09  N  18°♉  P 05    1985  05/19  N  29°♉  P 05
      11/02  S  09°♏  T 05          11/12  S  20°♏  T 05

1968  03/28  N  08°♈  P 06    1986  04/09  N  19°♈  P 06
      09/22  S  00°♎  T 06          10/03  S  10°♎  T 06

1969  03/18  N  28°♓  A 07    1987  03/29  N  08°♈  AT 07
      09/11  S  19°♍  A 07          09/23  S  00°♎  A 07

1970  03/07  N  17°♓  T 08    1988  03/18  N  28°♓  T 08
      08/31  S  08°♍  A 08          09/11  S  19°♍  A 08

1971  02/25  N  06°♓  P 09    1989  03/07  N  17°♓  P 09
      07/22  S  29°♋  P 09          08/31  S  08°♍  P 09
      08/20  S  27°♌  P 09
                               1990  01/26  N  07°♒  A 10
1972  01/16  N  25°♑  A 10          07/22  S  29°♋  T 10
      07/10  S  19°♋  T 10
                               1991  01/15  N  25°♑  A 11
1973  01/04  N  14°♑  A 11          07/11  S  19°♋  T 11
      06/30  S  09°♋  T 11
      12/24  N  03°♑  P 12    1992  01/04  N  14°♑  A 12
                                     06/30  S  09°♋  T 12
1974  06/20  S  29°♊  T 12          12/24  N  02°♑  P 13
      12/13  N  21°♐  P 13
                               1993  05/21  S  01°♊  P 13
1975  05/11  S  20°♉  P 13          11/13  N  22°♏  P 14
      11/03  N  10°♏  P 14
                               1994  05/10  S  20°♉  A 14
1976  04/29  S  09°♉  A 14          11/03  N  11°♏  T 15
      10/23  N  00°♏  T 15
                               1995  04/29  S  09°♉  A 15
1977  04/18  S  28°♈  A 15          10/24  N  00°♏  T 16
      10/12  N  19°♎  T 16
                               1996  04/17  S  28°♈  P 16
1978  04/07  S  17°♈  P 16          10/12  N  20°♎  P 17
      10/02  N  09°♎  P 17
                               1997  03/09  S  19°♓  T 17
1979  02/26  S  07°♓  T 17          09/01  N  10°♍  P 18
      08/22  N  29°♌  T 18
                               1998  02/26  S  08°♓  T 18
1980  02/16  S  27°♒  T 18          08/22  N  29°♌  A 19
      08/10  N  18°♌  A 19
                               1999  02/16  S  27°♒  A 19
1981  02/04  S  16°♒  A 19          08/11  N  18°♌  T 01
      07/31  N  08°♌  T 01
```

Longitudes of Major Fixed Stars

DIFDA	1Ar53	CAPHIR	9Li27
ALGENIB	8 28	ALGORAB	12 45
ALPHERATZ	13 37	SEGINUS	16 58
BATEN KAITOS	21 15	FORAMEN	21 35
AL PHERG	26 7	SPICA	23 9
VERTEX	27 8	ARCTURUS	23 32
MIRACH	29 42	PRINCEPS	2Sc27
SHARATAN	3Ta16	KHAMBALIA	6 10
HAMAL	6 58	ACRUS	11 11
ALMACH	13 32	ALPHECCA	11 35
MENKAR	13 37	SOUTH SCALE	14 23
CAPULUS	23 30	NORTH SCALE	18 40
ALGOL	25 28	UNUKALHAI	21 22
ALCYONE	29 18	AGENA	23 6
PRIMA HYADUM	5Ge 6	BUNGULA	28 51
ALDEBARAN	9 5	YED PRIOR	1Sg36
RIGEL	16 8	ISIDIS	1 52
BELLATRIX	20 15	GRAFFIAS	2 29
CAPELLA	21 10	HAN	8 32
PHACT	21 28	ANTARES	9 4
MINTAKA	21 40	RASTABAN	11 16
EL NATH	21 53	SABIK	17 16
ENSIS	22 22	RASALHAGUE	21 45
ALNILAM	22 46	LESATH	23 19
AL HECKA	24 5	ACULEUS	25 4
POLARIS	27 52	ACUMEN	28 0
BETELGEUZE	28 3	SINISTRA	29 3
MENKALINAN	29 13	SPICULUM	29 57
TEJAT	2Cn44	POLIS	2Cp31
DIRAH	4 36	FACIES	7 37
ALHENA	8 24	PELAGUS	11 41
SIRIUS	13 24	ASCELLA	12 56
CANOPUS	14 14	MANUBRIUM	14 18
WASAT	17 49	WEGA	14 37
PROPUS	18 16	DENEB	19 6
CASTOR	19 33	TEREBELLUM	25 8
POLLUX	22 32	ALBIREO	0Aq33
PROCYON	25 6	ALTAIR	1 4
PRAESAEPE	6Le32	GIEDI	3 7
N. ASELLUS	6 51	DABIH	3 21
S. ASELLUS	8 1	OCULUS	4 1
ACUBENS	12 57	BOS	4 28
ALGENUBI	20 0	ARMUS	12 2
ALPHARD	26 35	DORSUM	13 9
ADHAFERA	26 52	CASTRA	19 30
AL JABHAH	27 12	NASHIRA	21 5
REGULUS	29 8	SADALSUUD	22 42
ZOSMA	10Vi37	DENEB ALGEDI	22 50
DENEBOLA	20 55	SADALMELIK	2Pi39
COPULA	24 23	FOMALHAUT	3 9
LABRUM	25 55	DEEB ADIGE	4 38
ZAVIJAVA	26 27	SKAT	8 10
MARKEB	28 12	ACHERNAR	14 36
ZANIAH	4Li 8	MARKAB	22 47
VINDEMIATRIX	9 15	SCHEAT	28 41

Medical Bibliography

Boles. "Transcripts of the AMA Annual Meetings."

Cornell, H.L. *Encyclopedia of Medical Astrology.* St. Paul, MN: Llewellyn, 1972.

Fabricant, N.D. "Otolaryngology and the Weather." *Illinois Medical Journal* 78:511-515, December 1940.

Forbes, W.H.; D.B. Dill; and F.G. Hall. "Effects of Climate upon Volumes of Blood and Tissue Fluid in Man." *American Journal of Physiology* 130:734-756, October 1940.

"Hemodynamic Changes in Dogs in Relation to the Autonomic Nervous System." 77070, 1956.

Kelley, D.M., "Mania and the Moon." *Psychoanalyst Review.* 29:406-426, October 1942.

Kety, S.S., "Blood Flow and Metabolism of the Human Brain in Health and Disease" *Transactions and Studies of the College of Physicians.* 18:103-108, December 1950.

Kinkade, J.M. "Climatologic Factors in Ears, Nose and Throat Diseases" *Laryngoscope* 63:311-320, April 1953.

Max, L.W. "Experimental Study of Motor Theory of Consciousness: Action-Current Responses in Deaf-Mutes During Sleep, Sensory Stimulation and Dreams." *Journal of Comparative Psychology* 19:486-489, June 1935.

McDaniel, W.B. "The Moon, Werewolves, and Medicine." *Transactions and Studies of the College of Physicians.* 18:113-122, December 1950.

Peterson, W.F. "The Patient and the Weather." Vols. 1-5. Ann Arbor: Ann Arbor Press, 1934-1938.

Preston, B.S. "Lure of Legendary Medicine." *Western Virginia Medical Journal.* 32:32-39, January 1936.

Utrata, J. "Postoperative Hemorrhages Related to Atmospheric Changes." *AMA Archives of Otolaryngology 67:215-218, February 1958.*

Bibliography

Berne, Eric. *The Games People Play.* New York: Grove Press, 1964.

Brown, F.W., Jr. "Rhythmic Nature of Animals and Plants." *Northwestern University Tri-Quarterly* 1:35, Fall 1958.

Dhi Manthri, Chandra. *The Degrees of Life.* Van Nuys, CA: Astro-Analytics, 1976.

Eclipses: 1865-2000 A.D. American Federation of Astrologers, 1960.

Harris, Thomas A. *I'm Okay—You're Okay.* New York: Harper & Row, 1969.

Jansky, Robert Carl. "The Eclipse as a Tool in Prediction" *Astrology Now,* January 1976.

——*Getting Your Correct Birth Data.* Van Nuys, CA: Astro-Analytics, 1975.

Jayne, Charles A. *A New Dimension in Astrology: Nodes, Eclipses & Other Alignments.* Monroe, NY: Astrological Bureau, 1975.

Kolisko. "The Moon and Growth of Plants."

Mayo, Jeff. *The Planets in Human Behavior.* London: Fowler, 1972.

Nelson, J.H. *Cosmic Patterns: Their Influence on Man and his Communication.* American Federation of Astrologers, 1974.

Robertson, Marc. *The Transit of Saturn.* Seattle, WA: The Astrology Center of the Northwest, 1973.

Sepharial. *Eclipses.* North Hollywood, CA: Signs & Symbols, 1973.

Sheehy, Gail. *Passages.* New York: E.P. Dutton, 1974.

True Lunar Nodes: 1850-2000. Ithaca, NY, Digicomp Research Corporation, 1975.